You Can't Get To Heaven Wearing Tight Shoes

A Book About
Personal Honesty

Patricia St. E. Darlington, Ph.D.

Llumina Press

Cover art and illustrations by Whitney Pollett: www.whitneypollett.com

Unless otherwise noted all bible references/quotes were taken from the following bibles:

Holy Bible: New Living Translation. (1996). Tyndale House Publishers, Inc. Weaton, IL.

The Amplified Bible: Containing the Amplified Old Testament and the Amplified New Testament. (1987). Zondervan Bible Publishers, Grand Rapids, MI.

Unless otherwise noted all quotes used in this book were taken from the websites listed below:
www.blogs.princeton.edu
www.thinkexist.com
www.wisdomquotes.com/cat_hypocrisy.html

ISBN: 978-1-60594-596-5 (PB)

Printed in the United States of America by Llumina Press

Library of Congress Control Number: 2010911223

Contents

Dedication

This book is lovingly dedicated to Bishop Darlington, our adorable Mini Schnauzer who transitioned February 2010.
Bishop, you were the most completely honest being I have ever known.

I miss you in my shadow as I walk.

Acknowledgements

There are many to whom I owe an immense debt of gratitude for this book. First, I give my gratitude to my husband, Headley, who listened to a new idea every day and nodded with patience, love, and an ever-present, indulgent smile, even when his mind was obviously elsewhere and he had no idea what I was prattling on about. Nose rubs of love and gratitude to my daughter Rolda, the Golden Goddess, who loved the concept, showed her enthusiasm and honesty by telling me to rewrite the book, and then proceeded to help me do just that. Thanks to my son Headley, my Golden Light, who gave me many shoulder rubs and often took me out to see a movie to break the tension. Thank you to my son Bashir, my Golden Muse who always inspires me to create.

I extend my deepest gratitude to my friend, counselor, and critic, Rhonda Rowland, who loved the idea for the book from the first day, egged me on to stay put when I slowed up on the writing, and reined me in when I tried to jump ahead to the next idea for the next book—I miss you. To my friends Karen (East-Jacobs-Moran-East) Lopez and Laura Ostberg; my stress relief posse and fellow members of the Wild Women's Poker Club, I acknowledge my love and gratitude for reading every word of the unedited version and taking me off to fabulous weekends with endless rounds of Tequila and Sea Breezes—sorry for the pain. Thank you to my friend Joe Worndle, missionary extraordinaire, who assured me that this book was written for guys as well as girls. I am also grateful to my friend, Judi Hamilton, for reading a very rough draft and trying so hard to put me in the right places to get the book noticed.

Finally, to those who actually helped to take my idea from fantasy to reality, I extend my deepest thanks. These folks include my friend and colleague, Walter Burton, who succeeded in putting me in the right place with the right person. I extend my forever gratitude to my new friend and colleague, Gerry Czarnecki, who turned out to be the right person, in the right place, and who came armed with an extraordinary amount of honesty. Gratitude to my old friend and new publisher, Deborah Greenspan, at Llumina Press, who ultimately was the right person, in the right place, at the right time. Thank you to my friend and publicist, Michelle Brown, at Kaliah Communications who agreed to work for free until . . . , and to Dale Rosenberg, the toughest and most persnickety but warm-hearted editor any writer has ever encountered; thanks a lot for making me cry—tears of joy!

✦

ജ്ഞ

From the viewpoint of Reality, it [evil]* is an illusion, but they have not denied it as an experience. It is an experience all have had. The great have not failed to recognize the *appearance* of evil, but they have separated the appearance from reality. They have done away with evil as a cosmic entity—NO DEVIL, NO HELL, NO TORMENT, NO DAMNATION outside of one's own state of thought, NO PUNISHMENT outside of that self-inflicted, through ignorance; and NO SALVATION OUTSIDE OF CONSCIOUS CO-OPERATION WITH THE INFINITE. *Heaven and Hell are states of consciousness.*

Ernest Holmes

The Science of Mind: A Philosophy, A Faith, A Way of Life

*Brackets added

Preface

As a young girl growing up in an extreme Pentecostal heritage, I had very definite knowledge and opinions on the day-to-day workings of that place called hell. I knew exactly what it took and how easy it was to get there. I must admit, however, that I wasn't sure what it took to stay out. I grew up on an island with an average daily temperature just shy of what I am sure would make the first few levels of hell seem like the Arctic. As a young person, I was absolutely certain that I, and most of the people I knew, would all end up in hell. You see, current wisdom (I am really not sure where this particular bit of wisdom came from) had it that we were all born sinners and could never really hope to be redeemed until we had perhaps died a few times and had learned to be better persons in each lifetime. With my smart mouth and bad attitude, it was pretty clear that I was doomed to go around the circuit for an eternity and still end up in that very hot place.

I also grew up with the understanding (I have never been clear from where this came either) that there was this really big angel with a very Big Book who recorded my evil deeds, so he could use them against me on the day I tried to gain entrance into the heavenly realm. This big angel and I were never on good terms since there was just too much recording to be done where I was concerned. His constant companion was a really little dude with a gadget, which I named a "Sin O'Meter." My relationship with the Little Guy was equally strained. In my mind, he looked like a gnome with really bad teeth. This gnome-like character insisted on flashing his gruesome little teeth every time he tallied up a few more infractions to be added to my record. You see, sins seemed to lie everywhere I went. It appears that the sins were just waiting for me to pass by, so they could jump out and attach themselves to me.

My mother was the owner of a very large and extremely sensitive instrument, which I named her "Sin Geiger Counter." She and her machine seemed constantly poised to spot every one of the sins which apparently attached themselves to me like neon lights. Not a day went by when I wasn't found guilty of breaking at least one of what I began to refer to as the ten biblical "Thou Shalt Nots," aka the Ten Commandments. Rumor has it that when I wasn't busy running around looking for Thou Shalt Nots to break, I was on a quest to commit one or more of Pope St. Gregory the Great's "Seven Deadly Sins." It finally got to the point where I decided that I was completely irredeemable and bound to burn. You know what they say, "If you are going to do the time, you might as well do the crime," and boy, did I!

This strategy worked for a while until I think even the Big Guy and the Little Guy got sick of me. For a long time, I had nightmares of them throwing the Big Book and the Sin O'Meter at me and telling me to go to hell. Finally, I was left on my own to sink or swim, and I decided to just do what I felt was best for me regardless of what anyone else thought. That's when it happened. I began to care much more about my own feelings and much less about anyone else's Big Book, Sin O'Meter, or Sin Geiger Counter. I'd finally had enough. I ditched the arbitrary judgments of the Big Guy with the Big Book, my mother with her Sin Geiger Counter, and the Little Guy with The Sin O'Meter for the kinder, gentler cautions of my own "Personal Honesty Meter." I quit trying so hard to be perfect and decided to become real.

Free at last, free at last . . .

In my quest to figure it all out, I began a period of intense study on the subject of religion, spirituality, heaven, hell, and sin. The universe, as it always does when we seek in earnest, provided all the answers that I needed to my questions. One of the first answers I received was to the question "what does it mean to commit a sin?" The answer I got came from the early Greek translation of the word for sin, *hamartia,* as "missing the mark." I began to learn that heaven and hell were of my own making and that by committing a sin, I was simply "missing the mark" of what was right and what was wrong. I soon realized that all I had to do was do my best and do so honestly. I found out then and there that I held the keys to heaven in the palms of my hands. I also decided that the only sins I had committed were those that made me feel and know, in my heart and soul, that I had "missed the mark." I began to recognize that I missed the mark when my actions, immediately or upon reflection, made me feel less than wholesome, less than loving, less than joyful, lacking in bliss and contentment, less than honest, and ultimately, devoid of happiness.

Finally, I decided that I was the one who needed to examine myself and determine my rating on my own "Personal Honesty Meter." Once I could look inside, see what was there, and feel love and joy for myself and others, I "found the mark" and achieved heaven here on earth. I also decided that the list of Thou Shalt Nots and the plethora of Deadly Sins were to be used by me, and me alone, to help me keep my moral compass. No big angel could, or would, hold the Big Book of my salvation and use it against me. No Little Guy could turn his Sin O'Meter on me and have it shriek in indignation. My mother's Sin Geiger Counter could no longer alert her or anyone else to my infractions. I was fully capable of using those guideposts myself. All I needed to do was to be conscious, aware, and personally honest. My heaven existed for me to occupy.

Rocky Road is not always ice cream

Oh, but did I just say "all I needed . . . ?" Surely you knew that there had to be a catch. Did anyone ever teach you to be cautious of people who start out by telling you, "Oh, don't worry, all you need . . ." Well, no difference here, because, you see, all we need to do now is to figure out how to talk the talk and walk the walk on the pathway to a life built on a foundation of personal honesty. Believe me when I tell you that quite often it is a rocky road.

You see, that "all you need" part is a doozy when it comes to personal honesty. What they forgot to tell us, dear ones, is that it isn't as easy as it looks or sounds. Tell me, have you ever tried being *completely* honest? Girls, it's almost as hard as working at the Cheesecake Factory and trying to lose weight! Guys, it's twice as hard as growing back hair in that little bald spot on the top that seems perfectly positioned to reflect the light across the room if you forget to wear your newest baseball cap. It's almost as hard as covering up cigarette breath with Mentos AND Altoids (consumed in counts of threes and all at the same time). I have it on good authority that being personally honest is three times harder than giving the waitress back the thirty-three dollars change she gave you from the twenty dollar bill you gave her. Folks, take it from someone who knows, this journey we are about to go on is no piece of cake. But I never promised you a walk in the park, did I? Instead let's just a stroll through one of our favorite stores in the mall, the shoe store. Taking this trip is guaranteed to land us squarely inside our personal heaven here on earth.

By now you must be asking yourself, "What in the name of all the saints does personal honesty have to do with wearing tight shoes?" The answer, my friend, is this: personal honesty has everything to do with it, and I will demonstrate this shortly. But first, let me make a few confessions—you know, they say it's good for the soul. I use the Christian Bible as, among other things, a tool to develop discipline. That's right. I have read the bible from Genesis to Revelation, word for word, every year for the past several years. To be honest, it takes a tremendous amount of willpower, determination, discipline and at least some small fondness for misery and torture, to actually read through what I have jokingly come to call the "begats." That is, Abraham begat Isaac, and Isaac begat Jacob, and Jacob begat Joseph, and Joseph begat … and so on and so forth. Get it? Believe me when I say there was an awful lot of "begetting" going on in biblical times!

Second, I will be very candid and say that I did not undertake this ritual because I am vying for a chance to be named a saint. My mother, in an obvious state of post partum delusion or wishful thinking, already granted me that privilege[1]. Nor do I do it because I consider myself some sort of above-average Christian. I am not. On the contrary, I have read the Bible through and through, page by page, word by word, a new bible every year, in an attempt to develop discipline and, yes, to keep myself personally honest. After all, who else would ever know if I skipped over a begat or two? The answer is, I would know. And why is this important? It's important because, for me, there is an even bigger, and what I consider more important issue: If I could ever consider lying to myself, how could I then expect to be honest with others?

Another truth about my relationship with the bible is that I have developed a fondness for this incredible text, which seems to be an amazing compilation of wisdom words. It encompasses the teachings of virtue, ethics, and morals that are found in most, if not all, of our religious and spiritual traditions. It is perhaps the most widely read amalgam of mythology, allegory, metaphor, symbolism, and yes, even contradictions, to which most of us have been exposed, even if we do not actually follow all of its tenets. And, frankly, despite the fact that all of the moral attributes referred to in this book are found in almost every other fundamental religious or spiritual teaching, it is the one with which I am most familiar.

---

[1] For those of you who might be of the curious/nosy variety, the St. in my name is actually an abbreviation for "Saint."

On the other hand, for those among us who may not be advocates or admirers of anything religious or spiritual, and may therefore find no resonance with the Bible and the Ten Commandments, I sincerely hope you didn't think you were going to get off scot-free. I have just the thing for you: a way to view the commandments from a slightly different perspective. Let me direct your attention to any law book and have you peruse the laws of most of the western world. You may be quite surprised to discover that most of what we have all been exposed to as our western "ways of living," are simply the result of a clever and, sometimes not so creative, repackaging of the Ten Commandments. We are all familiar with what can happen if you break the "laws" of the land and commit murder, adultery, steal, or lie (aka commit perjury). Does any of this sound familiar? Darn right it does. Keep in mind that while committing these acts may or may not be considered *sins* in our modern society, breaking these laws can, and often will, land you in the slammer, or at the very least, in a divorce court. From what I have heard, being in either of those places is a lot more like being in hell than in heaven. So, no matter what we choose to call them—commandments or laws—breaking them seems to come with consequences, either to society or to ourselves. Frankly, I would much rather answer to myself than to some judge or the Big Guy with the Big Book, hence the notion of *personal* honesty. Since, like myself, many of us are familiar with the Bible I chose this particular set of teachings as the foundation on which to base this discussion of personal honesty.

Introduction

"Honesty is the first chapter in the book of wisdom."

Thomas Jefferson

Friend 1: "Hey, it's me."

Friend 2: "I know it's you. The question is, where are you? You were supposed to be here twenty minutes ago."

Friend 1: "Oh, don't start."

Friend 2: "What do you mean, don't start? You're always late!"

Friend 1: "You know that's not true; I'm not always late."

Friend 2: "Ok, forgive me for lying. You're right; you're never late. You're just never on time."

Friend 1: "I can't believe you would say that about me. You know what? Just forget it."

Friend 2: "You know what? You're right. After all, you and the truth have never had much of an acquaintance. So, just tell me, are you on your way?"

Friend 1: "What do you mean, am I on my way? Of course, I'm on my way. As a matter of fact, I left home at least twenty minutes ago."

Friend 2: "Twenty minutes ago. As in two zero: twenty?"

Friend 1: "Yes, I'm fully aware that it's only a five minute drive. Yes, yes, I know what time it is. But it's not my fault that traffic is backed up for miles and miles. There must be a terrible accident somewhere up ahead. Can't you hear the sirens? Seriously, though, I left home in plenty of time to get to your place. Now, I'm just sitting in this parking lot of a highway."

Friend 2: "Exactly what is that noise?"

Friend 1: "What noise? I don't hear anything."

Friend 2: "I'm talking about the noise that sounds like the tea kettle I gave you for Christmas."

Friend 1: "Oh, no, no, no, umm, that's not my tea kettle you're hearing. Oh, wait a minute, that must be the fire truck that just whizzed by me on the way to the accident I told you about."

Friend 2: "I guess that barking in the background is the dog chasing the fire truck, right?"

Bambi: "Arf, arf."

Friend 1: "Barking? What barking in the background? How could you hear barking in the background?"

Friend 2: "Gosh, must be my lying ears playing tricks on me again."

Bambi: "Arf, arf."

Friend 1: "Well, I don't care what you say; that is not Bambi barking at the UPS man. You know you've been having that little hearing problem lately."

Bambi: "Arf, arf."

Friend 2: "I hear barking."

Friend 1: "Barking, for heaven's sake, stop with the barking! I told you I left home at least ten minutes ago. Now, can you please let me get off this phone? There's a cop behind me, and I don't want to get a ticket for talking on the phone and driving. Bye, bye. I've gotta go. I'm trying to merge, and you're gonna get me killed with all this talking."

"Whew, darn, that fool can talk! Bambi, you've just got to shut up when I'm on the phone, and for heaven's sake please leave that poor UPS man alone. Now, where is my wallet? Where in God's name did I put those blasted keys? Phew. Never thought I'd get out of that damn house. . . . Oh no, no, no. Please start, please, please, please start. Don't do this to me now. Not now, not today! Damn it. Now, how am I ever going to convince her that I left home on time? You know, I just have to change my ways and stop with this awful lying. It's bound to catch up with me one of these days."

Friend 1: "Hey Girl, it's me again. Do you think you could pick me up instead? Yeah, I know. It's a long story, but I'll fill you in when you get here. I have to tell you though, the tow truck guy who just picked me up on the side of the highway when my car overheated from sitting in that bad traffic jam—God, was he cute . . .!"

Bambi: "Arf, arf."

Ladies and gentlemen, friends and kinfolk, please raise your hand if you've ever found yourself in a situation similar to the scenario you just read. Okay, for those of us who are scrunching up our brows, shaking our heads vigorously from side to side in denial, and mumbling, "Never, ever, ever," please take note that I did not say *identical*; I simply said *similar.* Now, take a look at your sides. Hands still down? You mean you have never, ever told a little itty-bitty, teensy-weensy white lie? Never, ever? Really? Now what on earth is that awful smell? Kinda like something burning . . . Liar, liar, pants on fire.

For those of us who smiled guiltily and nodded as we remembered finding ourselves in a similar situation, or two, perhaps we can simply pray for our fellow goody-two-shoes friends and kin folks, and just think about what we can do to make a change in ourselves. Since, you know, that's really where it starts.

Growth and change: Why bother? Because it's good for us, that's why!

To grow is to change. But not all change is good. We all know that change is not always desired or welcome. We can also all acknowledge that change for the sake of change, or because someone forces us to change, is a waste of energy and generally, an exercise in futility. For change to be good, it needs to be proactive, conscious, personally desired and directed. Many times, maintaining the status quo is much preferred. Why bother when things seem to be going along just fine or, at the very least, are tolerable? Why rock the boat? Why muddy the water?

Well, take a moment to consider this. Just what do you want from this life? Just how much do you think you deserve? If your answers to those two questions are "nothing" and "nothing," then perhaps you should stop reading right now and pass this book along to the person whose answers are "everything" and "everything." Whoa! Did you actually pause and consider the questions I asked above or did you just plow right past them? Did you stop and take a minute to consider what it is you want from this life like I asked you to do? Honestly now. You see, this is a book about consciously and actively becoming aware of our actions and then possibly changing ourselves and our actions in a manner that will guarantee us a fulfilled, productive, and abundant life. It is about using the simplest of methods to create a life full of deliberate choices rather than choices made without consciousness or made inadvertently. The book is about being fully awake when we think, speak, and act. It is a book about developing our awareness of the things we say and do without thought. The book is about awareness of the behaviors and the attitudes that have become habitual from constant use, but which lack consciousness. It is a book that will help us to look at ourselves without judgment, but look nonetheless. It is about personal honesty and awareness.

Why awareness? Well, without awareness, knowledge is unfocused. Without awareness, knowledge is undirected. Having awareness without knowledge is like owning a car without knowing how to drive it or even what purpose the car serves. In this case, the car is a beautiful but useless luxury. The same holds true with the lessons in this book. Knowledge without awareness is useless. Our job then is to first create an *awareness* of the various and plentiful ways in which we practice personal dishonesty, generally with complete lack of consciousness or guile. Next, we provide *knowledge* concerning the ways in which we can begin to rethink our patterns with an aim to creating a change. This book is about practicing "right thinking."

Now, how does the very simple, even playful title of this book help us to practice right thinking? What does right thinking mean, exactly? Well, it means exactly what it says. We, at least many of us, consider heaven our ultimate reward for good behavior while we are here on earth. It really matters not whether we are considering heaven in a literal or figurative manner. The fact is that like Xerox, the word heaven has come to mean the same thing for most people who invoke it. That is, heaven is the just reward reserved for honest people!

So, if I say we can't get to heaven wearing tight shoes, I am suggesting there is something morally wrong with consciously and deliberately wearing shoes that are too small for your feet. Yes, I am stating unequivocally that the act of wearing tight shoes is not only physically damaging, but that wearing tight shoes damages your very soul! That's right. The same holds true for a lot of other things that we do, both with and without conscious thought.

For example, we lie about our jobs and then we lie, steal, and cheat at our jobs. We lie to our parents, our spouses, and our children, and then we lie to our neighbors about our parents, spouses, and children. We lie about love, and then we lie to our loved ones. We lie about sex, whether we're having it or not, and then we lie about how good we are at it. We lie about our low weight and our great health. Then we cheat when we eat; we cheat when we workout; and we lie about what size we wear. On and on we go, day in and day out.

Lying, cheating, even stealing have become universal pastimes. We seem to be doing it so much that we are even able to convince ourselves with our own lies. However, as we are all painfully aware, telling a little lie is like being a little bit pregnant; sooner or later, it leads to bigger things.

Here is a small question to ponder: To whom are we really lying? If we are all lying, and we suspect that everyone else is, who are we trying to fool but ourselves? Here is a bigger question: What is this really doing to us? Have we become a people who are unable to even trust ourselves? If the answer to this question is yes, how do we begin to rebuild this trust? The answer lies with the difficult but necessary charge of taking the time to know and love ourselves.

To know, know, know me, is to love, love, love me . . .

I assure you that, as difficult a task as knowing and loving ourselves may seem, it is indeed doable, one day at a time. As you begin to contemplate the process of loving yourself, you will find out that a vital part of this process is developing personal honesty. There is an old song, *To Know You Is to Love You*, and I say, how can we or anyone else know us if we are constantly lying to ourselves and others about who we are? Further, how can you love someone whom you don't know? Honestly, you can't. You can, however, begin the process of knowing yourself by looking inside and allowing yourself to see the true you. This can be the first step in the process of developing a sense of personal honesty.

". . . and the truth shall make you free"

According to one of, if not *the* most quoted books of our time, Jesus, one of the great spiritual teachers, taught in John 8:32 that, "Ye shall know the truth, and the truth shall make you free." Also, according to another greatly quoted book, *Webster's Dictionary*, truth and honesty are synonyms. *Webster's Dictionary* expands its definition of the word honesty by noting that it implies a refusal to lie, steal, or deceive in any way. Honesty also includes behavior that is conducted without cheating, is genuine, real, reputable, respectable, good, worthy, creditable, praiseworthy, and marked with integrity.

All of these attributes are promoted in the teachings of religions and spirituality, and it is without question that there is immeasurable value to each and every one of them. But, with all the stumbling blocks that seem poised at the ready to derail us on our quest for right living, how do we ever attain what sometimes seem like insurmountable heights of goodness? Does any of this goodness really matter, or are we just wasting time pondering another imponderable like "Where did I come from?" or "Where am I going?" and "If I did decide to take this trip, do I even know how to get started?" Perhaps, one key to getting started on this journey is to first become acquainted with yourself in a very honest way. But you know it isn't all that easy.

Just a spoonful of sugar . . .

Questions of personal honesty can be harsh medicine to swallow, so I have chosen to use just a tad of humor as the spoonful of sugar to help the medicine go down and, hopefully, in a most delightful way. Let us begin by returning for a moment to that often (mis)quoted book, the *King James Bible*, and start with the Commandments of Jesus to "love the Lord your God with all your heart and with all your soul and with all your mind," and to "love thy neighbor as thyself." Honestly now, how easy is it going to be for us to love our neighbors if we don't even love ourselves? We must acknowledge that it may be rather difficult to ask us to love the next door neighbor who keeps stealing our Sunday paper and letting their "Little Pookie" take a dump on our front lawn right by the mailbox. This is the same neighbor who is forever leaving his or her trash can directly behind our car so that we can back out over it at least once a week. Yet we're supposed to love them? If that is not hard enough, can we really be expected to love the neighbor who lives in another town, another state, another continent? You see, we have to come to terms with the idea that the word, neighbor, actually means every other being on this our home planet, and not just those pesky folks who were mean enough to take up residence at the address right next to us.

I recognize that, with this definition of the word neighbor in mind, Jesus might have been pushing his luck with the whole love thy neighbor as thyself bit, but, I believe there is hope. I do believe that there is a way to start the process, and it lies with each of us. As a matter of fact, I am going to go out on a limb and state emphatically that loving ourselves—warts, double chin, bald spot and all—is something that we can consciously, actively work on, and is a goal that we can actually achieve.

So let's begin with the process of loving ourselves by engaging in a little bit of personal honesty. But, let's make it fun! Let's start by looking inward and then around the corner! Let's start by looking at the little things we do that keep us mired in what you will soon come to know as the ten "Thou Shalt Nots" and "The Seven Deadlies," any one of which, if ignored or violated, seems guaranteed to keep us out of heaven, and slipping and sliding headfirst into hell, now or in the hereafter.

Part 1

"To Thine Own Self Be True . . ."

". . . And The Truth Shall Set You Free"

Chapter 1

To Thine Own Self Be True . . .

"To thine own self be true, and it must follow, as the night the day, thou canst not then be false to any man."

William Shakespeare

William Shakespeare wrote those words almost five hundred years ago, and they remain as true today as they were then. The admonition to be true to one's self, however, requires a level of personal honesty that can be difficult to achieve and that may prove to be easier to state than to actually do.

After all, let's face it. Ladies, when was the last time you gingerly tiptoed onto your bathroom scale, saw the extra five pounds you had packed on, and didn't immediately blame it on temporary water retention and bloating, rather than on the binge drinking or chocolate madness that you indulged in over the past couple of weeks? Gentlemen, how about you? We all know that the extra ten pounds that recently showed up on the bathroom scale are pure muscle from all that working out you've been doing lately, right? Surely, the pounds couldn't possibly be from all the nachos, beer, and chicken wings you consumed during the last football season, baseball season, Texas Hold Em season, or whatever season it is on TV. Folks, how long has it been since you promised your mom and dad that you would be over for a visit on the weekend, failed to show up because you carelessly made other plans, and then, without a great deal of thought, blamed it on the awful boss who asked you to work extra hours on the weekend?

Friends, these examples may appear as small, simple alterations in fact. However, when looked at cumulatively, and through a different prism, we may begin to realize that they have actually become small craters in our landscape of personal honesty. These craters may soon become a large reflection of all the dishonest acts that seem to tag along beside us day after day.

But what makes a dishonest act a dishonest act? Is it the size of the act, or the impact the act may have? Is it just the sheer occurrence of the event? The answer is probably relative to each individual. Each of us, however, if we can claim any fraction of a conscience, will soon come to realize that we actually have our own Personal Honesty Meter. This Personal Honesty Meter is the scale that allows us to determine if we can trust ourselves regardless of who else may or may not trust us. This is the measure that allows us to face ourselves in the mirror, smile, and continue to look rather than turn away with a scowl. It is this scale that assures us that we can confidently move forward in the quest toward achieving a satisfying, fulfilled, and abundant life; that is, if one is indeed working toward achieving a life built on a foundation of wisdom, honesty, and integrity.

But let's face it. How many times do we forget this caution and attempt to lie to ourselves and others? For many of us, this behavior has become such a habit that it no longer even registers as dishonesty. Here is an example. A friend calls and asks us to meet for a drink and a chat. Generally, our first response, if allowed to surface, is the one coming from our inner core. I believe this response is based on an innate desire for personal honesty. It would go something like this, "You know something (insert so-called best friend's name here), I am just too darn exhausted to move from this sofa and, frankly, I am sick and tired of listening to your whining, and if I had looked at the darn caller ID, I would never have picked up the phone. So (insert so-called best friend's name here), why don't you go get a life and leave me the hell alone?" Harsh? Yes, definitely. Honest? Yes, most definitely.

Instead, our actual response, the one based on our desire to present a front for others to see, is the one that comes from a place of complete dishonesty. You hear yourself saying, "Oh (insert so-called best friend's name here), I am so very sorry (no you are not!). You know I'd love to meet you (hell no, you wouldn't). It's been so long, and I can't wait to catch up (yeah, right). But you know what? I just walked in the door, and I have to turn around and go back to the office to pick up some papers that I left at . . . ummm . . . Starbucks. I really need those papers to finish a project that was due last week. Then I have to stop by the drugstore to pick up some medicine for Mom (who is out of town on vacation and has never been sick a day in her life), and then I have to run by the dry cleaners to pick up Dad's shirt (the shirt he took when he went on vacation with Mom). And you know what? I just realized that the poor dog (who passed last February) is out of dog food. And then I simply must . . . But you know what? I looked at the caller ID and saw that it was you, and I just had to pick up!"

Who wants to count how many lies, little bitty, teensy-weensy, white or otherwise, we just told? Instead, we could have kept our souls clean and sparkly by being personally honest and simply telling the plain, horrible, unvarnished, painful truth. "Thanks, but you know what? Let me be honest. I barely managed to make it into the house, and I am practically on my knees. My eyes have gone slightly blind, my jaws hurt from being clenched so much, and my neck and back are killing me." To this your kind friend may respond, "Oh dear, you sound awful, is there anything I can do? Do you need to get to the hospital? Can I call an ambulance for you?" Your pain-laden response? "Thank you so much, but the truth is, I don't think I can take another step. You see, I was in the mall the other day and I saw this heavenly pair of shoes. You know, I saw right off that they were just a tad too small, but I had to get them. I thought that with a little bit of stretching, I could make them work, and I wore them to work today. But after walking around all day trying to look cute in a pair of size seven shoes on my size nine feet, I spent the better part of the day in hell. I think I lost my left big toe and my right pinky toe sometime around lunch time, but I'm not sure since the blasted pair of shoes completely cut off the circulation in my toes. Now my ankles are swollen, my legs have turned black and blue, and I can feel a serious pain shooting up my backside, not to mention that I am going to need a crowbar and twenty minutes to pry them off. You know, its' got to be a sin to wear tight shoes." Now what's wrong with that answer? God bless our souls!

A couple of other questions need to be asked here, and they are; "Does any of this really matter?" "Who really cares about these small acts of dishonesty?" Well, I suggest that each of us must determine our own responses to these questions. There certainly is no ultimate "Personal Honesty Arbiter" standing ready to meter out rewards or punishment to us. The only judge of our character and integrity is ourselves. So, the desire to answer these questions is strictly individual and personal.

Now, many individuals may never even have chosen to ask the questions in the first place, and for those, this book may serve only to bring the issues into consciousness. For others, choosing to read this book may actually serve as a means of bringing into awareness your need to explore your own issues of personal honesty. Regardless of the intent for exploring this book, the information can serve to bring us all into a place of recognition, growth, and change, but only if we choose to let it. But where can we go to begin the process? The Mall I tell you, the mall, where I promise you will find out what wearing tight shoes has to do with getting into heaven.

Chapter 2

Mall Madness and that Den of Iniquity Called the "Shoe Store."

You Can't Get To Heaven Wearing Tight Shoes!

Why?

Let's Be Honest . . .

. . . 'cause you've lied, stolen, lusted, and coveted so much they might not even be willing to let you into hell.

In keeping with the importance of having a strong level of personal honesty, let us become acquainted, or for some of us backsliders, reacquainted, with what I believe are some of the most interesting passages ever written. I truly believe that these passages were designed to help us maintain a heightened level of *personal* honesty. I referred to them earlier as the Thou Shalt Nots. Yes, dear folks, I am referring to those Thou Shalt Nots given to Moses during one of his side trips up the mountain to meet with God while on his way with the children of Israel down to the Promised Land.

By the way, a quick side note before we move on. I myself must take a trip down the personal honesty highway and make an admission. This quick pause is in keeping with my desire for full disclosure. To be honest, and if you want to be truly picky like my friend Joe W., you may quibble with me and claim that there really are only eight Thou Shalt Nots listed in the Ten Commandments. The remaining are actually two Thou Shalts. However, for pure dramatic flair and my own pleasure—after all, it is my book, and I get to do what I want, no?—I have taken the liberty and chosen to reword the two Thou Shalts and make them work for me. Hence, "Thou shalt remember the Sabbath day to keep it holy" will now read, "Thou Shalt Not forget the Sabbath day by forgetting to keep it holy . . . ," and "Thou Shalt honor your father and your mother that your days may be long upon the land" will now read, "Thou Shalt Not dishonor your father and your mother . . . ." Amen. So, now that we are all on the same page, chapter and verse, nitpickers and all, let's spend a moment and take a really good look at the ten Thou Shalt Nots roughly summarized from Genesis 20: 3-17, to include the following admonitions:

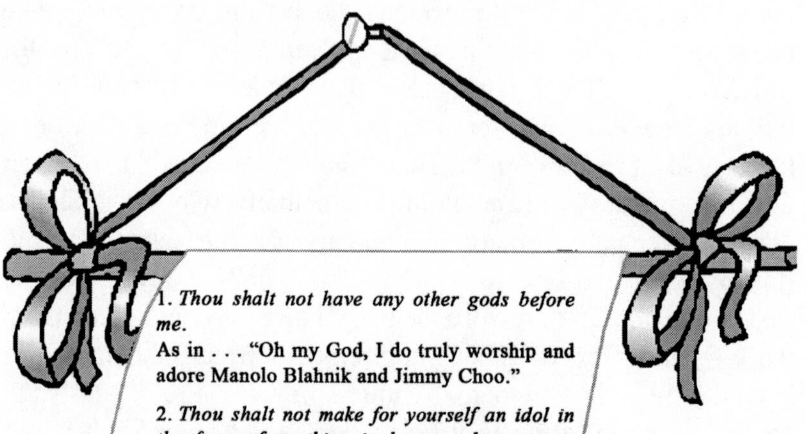

1. *Thou shalt not have any other gods before me.*
As in . . . "Oh my God, I do truly worship and adore Manolo Blahnik and Jimmy Choo."

2. *Thou shalt not make for yourself an idol in the form of anything in heaven above or on earth beneath or in the waters below. Thou shalt not bow down to them or worship them.*
As in . . . the $5,000 shoe closet you couldn't afford but had built anyway to hold the 100 pairs of shoes you own, and that you stand in front of with a rapturous gaze whenever you get the chance.

3. *Thou shalt not misuse the name of the Lord your God.*
As in . . . "Oh Dear God or Sweet, Sweet little tiny baby Jesus, I would do anything, and I do mean anything to have those shoes."

4. *Thou shalt not forget the Sabbath day by forgetting to keep it holy. For on the seventh day, you shall not work.*
As in . . . doing overtime on Saturday or Sunday to pay for the shoes you knew you couldn't afford to buy and the closet you couldn't afford to build in the first place.

5. *Thou shalt not dishonor your father and your mother.*
As in . . . "I would sell my mother to get those shoes," or "Dad, can I have a little extra money to meet my rent this month?" Money which you promptly send to the credit card company or, worse yet, take to the shoe store!

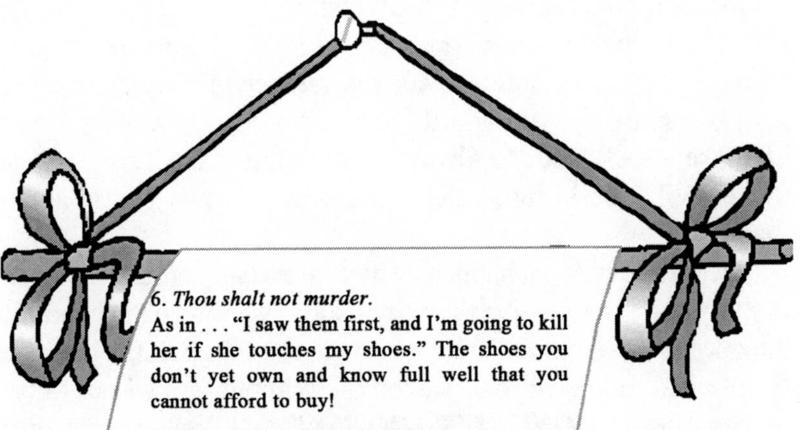

6. *Thou shalt not murder.*
As in . . . "I saw them first, and I'm going to kill her if she touches my shoes." The shoes you don't yet own and know full well that you cannot afford to buy!

7. *Thou shalt not commit adultery.*
As in . . . "Oh, your divorce is going to be final when? Good, because well, you see there are these shoes . . .

8. *Thou shalt not steal*
As in . . . using your Citibank credit card or your debit card to buy the shoes when you know you are over your limit and you have no money in the bank.

9. *Thou shalt not give false testimony*
As in . . . lying to the man on the phone that you mailed the check for the credit card payment yesterday, or trying to convince the people at the bank that you really did make an ATM deposit to your checking account after two o'clock last evening.

10. *Thou shalt not covet your neighbor's house, or his shoes, or his wife, or his ass, or his wife's ass.*
As in . . . Oh well, you get the picture, right?

(See Appendix 1 for an Easy Reference Guide to the Ten Commandments)

By now, I am sure that you have come to realize that just a simple, innocent trip past a shoe store could be the defining act that keeps us out of heaven. Horror of horrors, it gets worse. You could actually consider *entering* that shoe store and, worse of all, you could even consider *purchasing* a pair of those shoes that are always tantalizingly displayed inside those evil, sparklingly clean glass windows! Think about that!

Dear friends, what happens when we actually enter that den of iniquity and discover that the pair of shoes we saw in the window, the ones that we immediately knew owned our soul, the ones we simply had to have or could even die without, turned out to be, as they often are, ***ONE SIZE TOO SMALL?!*** What is to become of your tender soul? How could you possibly survive? I say to you now, as one who cares deeply about your redemption: run, flee, make a mad dash for the door. And for those of you who are of the Judeo-Christian persuasion, remember what happened to Lot's wife in Gen. 19:26 when she disobeyed and glanced back at all the good stuff—probably shoes—she thought she would be leaving behind. No family needs that much salt, so do not give so much as a backward glance. Escape for the sake of your very soul!!!

You see, what no one ever told us, is that: *"You Can't Get to Heaven Wearing Tight Shoes!"* What they, all those smarter than the average bear folks, failed to tell us, is that the one simple act of purchasing and attempting to wear a pair of tight shoes, covers enough of the Thou Shalt Nots to guarantee that they might not even be willing to let you into hell!

Let me elaborate. Consider Thou Shalt Not 9. This is the Thou Shalt Not that refers to *lying* (aka giving false testimony). Do you realize that by wearing tight shoes, you are lying about the size of your feet? That's right, my dear ones. You see, there is a real difference, pain wise, between a pair of size 9 shoes and a pair of size 10 shoes, especially in the cold Arctic temperatures of New York City in December or in the sweltering heat of South

Florida on any given day of the year. One temperature makes you swear with each step you take, and one makes you pray with each step you take. In neither case can you do it—your swearing or your praying—out loud since you will never be able to admit to anyone else where the source of your agony lies. Why? Well, that would confirm to all that you're a liar. And even worse, a liar with big feet!

And what about the Thou Shalt Not that refers to *stealing*? Never considered that one, did you? Well, by buying that pair of size 9 shoes and sticking your size 10 feet into them, you are actually stealing that pair of shoes from the rightful owner – the person with the true size 9 feet! And guess what? Remember the Thou Shalt Not that had to do with *coveting* your neighbor's significant other or his ass or whatever? Well, I am here to tell you, that also includes his or her shoe size. Yup, another major moral infraction committed without thought. And the commandment that says Thou Shalt Not *kill*? I am pretty sure that one is covered by the statement you made as you walked by the store display, spotted the pair of size 6 shoes always tantalizingly displayed, and droolingly uttered the words, "I would kill to get my feet into those shoes!" And wait just a minute. Isn't there some kind of mischief-making having to do with *Lust*? But no, that's not one of the ten Thou Shalt Nots is it? That comes with a later list of infractions. I am hoping that by now, the point has been made. But I am by no means finished. Rest assured, however, there is light at the end of the tunnel.

It is with immense relief and sincere gratitude that I inform you that the bible is not just chock-full of Thou Shalt Nots, despite the fact that there seems to be an awful lot of them. Actually, my absolute favorite part of the bible comes from what I fondly refer to as the "Thou Shalts," or the "Jesus Saids." I am talking about the part in Matt. 22: 37-39 where Jesus teaches us:

1. ***Thou shalt love the Lord your God with all your heart and with all your soul and with all your mind.***

(As in . . . "I know I can't afford those shoes this week, but I love the Lord, the Lord loves me and would want me to have those shoes, so I will pray on it, and the good Lord will provide a way.")

2. ***Thou shalt love your neighbor as yourself.***

(As in . . . "I know she is wearing my shoes—the ones I couldn't afford to buy this week—but I feel joy and happiness for her as she walks by me and flaunts them in my face, and because I love her, I pray she doesn't fall and break her scrawny, wrinkly neck.")

(See appendix 4 for an Easy Reference Guide to Jesus' two Commandments)

Now, while we are on the subject of personal honesty, I must admit that, over the years, after reading these two commandments over and over and attempting to practice a more positive and affirmative life, I have come to the conclusion that I will work to my final day to replace the ten "Thou Shalt Nots" with the two "Thou Shalts." Perhaps I am just a lazy coward, but I have found that these two passages are so much easier to remember and so much more comforting to contemplate and live by. For the purpose of this book, however, we are going to lay the foundation of personal honesty, first with the ten Thou Shalt Nots, and end with the two Thou Shalts. No pain, no gain!

Still, it doesn't end there. We all know you can't possibly have a beginning and an end without a middle. And boy, is this middle a doozy! Remember those Seven Deadly Sins I mentioned earlier? Well, lo and behold! It appears that every time we break one of those Thou Shalt Nots, we may also be committing one of those Seven Deadly Sins, hereafter referred to as "Deadly Sin number so or so."

You simply cannot convince me that there is not some dastardly collusion afoot out there designed to get us into more and more trouble and to keep us out of heaven! So, with that in mind, what are the Seven Deadlies that seem poised at the ready to meter out spiritual justice? Well, here they are, those transgressions which are fatal to spiritual progress:

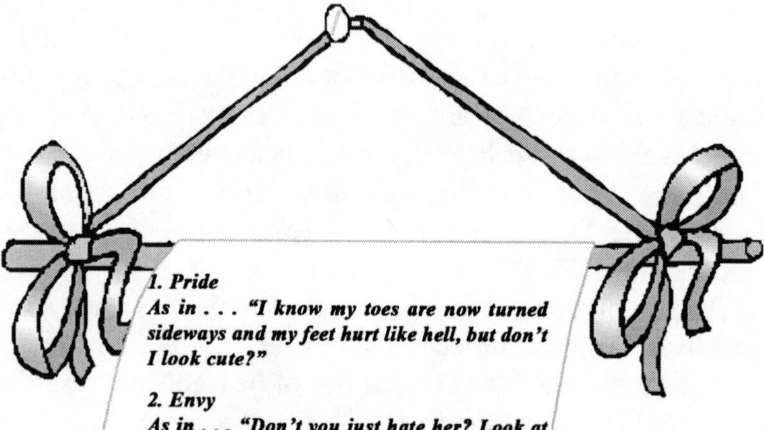

1. Pride
As in . . . "I know my toes are now turned sideways and my feet hurt like hell, but don't I look cute?"

2. Envy
As in . . . "Don't you just hate her? Look at those shoes, and you know she can't afford them on ten dollars an hour."

3. Gluttony
As in . . . "I know I already have that pair in six different colors, and I don't even know what color that is, but I want it anyway."

4. Lust
As in . . . "Oh my God, don't they just make you drool and tingle all over."

5. Anger
As in . . . "What do you mean they don't come in my size? Of course they come in my size. Now go back and check again or get me the manager."

6. Greed
As in . . . "Can I have one in every color, even if they don't fit?"

7. Sloth
As in . . . "I am so damn tired from all this walking and my feet hurt so badly from wearing these shoes, I can't even get up from this chair to get to the next shoe store."

(See Appendix 2 for an Easy Reference Guide to the Seven Deadly Sins)

So, just exactly where are these Thou Shalt Nots lurking, hiding and waiting to be violated? And where do the Deadly Sins hover, waiting to be committed? In the shoe store, I tell you. In the shoe store, and around every corner that you look! But we are here to help you find them and root them out. May the good Lord save our souls.

Now, this book, on the surface and because of its title, may appear to be a book designed to only help sinful women find their way into heaven. Gentlemen, this assumption would be completely incorrect. The truth of the matter is that there is good evidence to support the notion that we also can't get to heaven wearing shoes that are too *large* for our feet, no matter what the implications may be! So brothers, acknowledge your true shoe size, buy the size 8. Pay attention to the admonitions included in these pages, and I promise you that you too will greatly increase your likelihood of seeing the pearly gates! Now, let us look around the corner and see if we can up our chances!

Chapter 3

Health / Food / Fitness

You Mean They Actually Go Together?

You can't get to heaven eating fat-free cheesecake in front of your friends and loved ones!

Why?

Let's Be Honest . . .

. . . 'cause you misuse the name of the Lord when you ask yourself, "Gosh darn it, dag nab it, Dear Lord God Almighty, how can anyone actually eat that crap?"

♪♫ "Happy birthday to you, ♪♫ happy birthday to you, ♪♫ happy birthday dear *so and so*, ♪♫ happy birthday to you." ♪♫

As you clap your hands and grin widely to the gleeful sound of your well-wishers noisily issuing you up to another year of watching the clock move rapidly forward, you cringe inwardly. You feel the weight of impending depression creeping over you as you envision the numbers on the bathroom scale climbing upward with each passing year. Images of those numbers that seem to count down your life span tumble through your mind and you groan as your best friend helps you to slice into the giant, fat-free, sugar-free, taste-free cardboard mountain masquerading as your birthday cake.

Your friend hands you plate after plate as you cut slice after slice of this fluffy farce and pass it out to your friends and loved ones. You carefully scrutinize their expressions and note the look of horror that flashes over their faces before being quickly disguised by bright, cheery, smiles. You know what they're thinking. "She's the one who claims to be on a diet; why are we all suffering with her?" "Who eats fat-free cheese cake?" "How soon before we can respectfully say good-bye and get the hell out of here?"

You glance at your family, the ones who lovingly planned this wonderful birthday celebration with its exquisite array of flavored cardboard and sawdust passing as diet dishes. You know just how much they paid for this monstrosity of a confection and recognize that they did it out of love for you. You cringe as you acknowledge that they did it simply because you chose to begin your slippery slide down the steep slopes to hell. You did this when you created the entire charade and broke Thou Shalt Not 9 by giving false testimony about being on a diet and trying to eat right.

It is then that you break Thou Shalt Not 3, as you misuse the name of the Lord when you ask yourself, "Gosh darn it, dag nab it, Dear Lord God Almighty, how can anyone actually eat that crap?" Then, as you serve up the last slice of breath-stopping displeasure, and your friend passes it on to the next unsuspecting victim, you ask yourself, "Lord, how soon before I can respectfully say good-bye and get the hell out of this nightmare?" forgetting that this was all brought on by your own dishonesty.

Finally, after all the wisecracks about denture adhesive and protective undergarments, your cadre of loving friends and family beat their hasty retreat. You wander around your apartment glancing at the gifts piled high on the tables and chairs, and a feeling of emptiness floats over you and settles in your midsection—exactly where a huge bowl of luscious ice cream should be digesting right now—if only you had not wasted valuable time participating in that charade. You close your eyes and start to salivate at the thought of ice cream—thick, rich, sweet, dairy-filled cheesecake ice cream, a twofer, cheesecake and ice cream—that you have earned. It is an experience you need, a joy you must have if you are to live to see another nerve-racking birthday. Another year filled with rapidly graying eyebrows, graying armpit hairs and God forbid, graying . . . well, you know where. Then it hits you, and you know without a doubt, that the only thing that can save your life is a trip to the one place on earth where you can find solace at a time like this, the nearest Ice Cream Shoppe.

This is the place where you know you can find love. Within these walls, you can actually buy your cheesecake ice cream by the ton. You smile with glee as you ponder the fact that once there, you can make up for the farce you just pulled. My friend, it is there that you begin your rapid descent into hell. It is there that the third of the ten Thou Shalt Nots rears its ugly head again as you roll your eyes, grab your stomach and moan silently while you mouth the words, "God, dear God, sweet, sweet Jesus, Jesus, Jesus, did I die and go to heaven? 'cause look at what I just found!"

Then down goes Thou Shalt Not 2 as you start to fantasize about what shape your gluttonous (Deadly Sin 3), lustful (Deadly Sin 4), and greedy (Deadly Sin 6) concoction will take. Will it be one scoop or six? Will the scoops be nestled lovingly among bananas, cherries, nuts, and hot chocolate syrup? Or will they be sweetly blended in with crunchy, chewy nuts and raisins with a side of Oreo cookies just for fun? Momentarily, you lose yourself in this land of sugarplum fairies until your reverie is rudely interrupted by the sensation of a tissue brushing by you on a gentle but forceful breeze, and you open your eyes and take stock. Horror of horrors, you spy a teeny, tiny, twelve-inch-waist waif floating by to get ahead of you in line. Instantly, you feel anger (Deadly Sin 5) rumbling within as you lunge forward, intent on breaking Thou Shalt Not 6 as you murder this intruder.

As this apparition that passes for a woman glides past you, skips over the "Like it," "Love it," and settles on the "Gotta have it" wash-bucket-size of mind-numbing, earth-shattering, heavenly-bells-ringing gastronomical delight, you start to feel the tingly sensation of warm flickering flames rising up and gently licking against your feet. You take note of the intensifying heat as thoughts of envy (Deadly Sin 2) wash over you, and Thou Shalt Not 10 goes down in flames as you acknowledge just how much you covet your rival's ice cream consuming capacity.

Then she turns and offers you a gentle smile, and you recoil in horror as you notice them—her teeth—or rather what's left of them, and your heart sinks to the ground before it rises again and floats upward. You pull back from the cool glass counter where deadly pleasures beckon and you cast your eyes upward in gratitude for the lifeline that was just handed to you. You think to yourself, "I might be pleasingly plump, but at least I can smile about it." Then you lower your gaze and point to the tub of cheesecake ice cream and hold up one single finger in response to the server's cheery query of "How many scoops for you tonight?"

As you amble your way out of that corner of your heaven on earth, you think of the bullets you dodged tonight, and with a shudder, you recognize that a time of change is at hand. You know it won't be easy. You can begin the long, hard journey; however, by first forgiving yourself for having broken enough Thou Shalt Nots and for committing enough Deadly Sins to send you into purgatory for several lifetimes. You offer a special prayer for your parents' forgiveness for having broken Thou Shalt Not 5 when you dishonored them by lying to them (Thou Shalt Not 9) about your diet. Then the awareness of your situation settles over you like a mantle, and a calm reality sets in. Smiling with gratitude when you think about how you would have felt tomorrow morning if you had followed your instincts of gluttony (Deadly Sin 3) and greed (Deadly Sin 6) and allowed all of that dairy to find its way onto your nether regions. You know that you would have awakened feeling like a sloth (Deadly Sin 7), an awful feeling you have had many times before. But now you are joyful, resolving to make a change today. You could change your life right now.

Offering up a silent "hallelujah" as you pass slowly through the exit doors, you promise yourself that the next time you enter this heaven on earth you will be a different person. You will be a person in control of your desires. You will be a person who, through hard work and discipline, can look at yourself in the mirror and love the person you see looking back. You realize though that in order to get to the root of all your problems, you must first become vulnerable and expose yourself to a process of potentially painful but ultimately rewarding self examination based on pure personal honesty.

You make the decision to start the process and let the chips fall where they may. You start the process by wondering just what led to the lies, the sneaking around, and the feeling of never getting enough. You reflect on all the marks you missed during this period of separation from the real and perfect you. You remember the envy you experienced when you looked at others that you thought were so beautiful because of their smaller dress size, bust size, and even their shoe size. You recall the anger you struggled with when no one noticed that you had lost a pound or two. You vow to examine your life and your soul to find out what sent you to this dark place of self-loathing in the first place, that place that would make you abuse your body with food, then diet, then food abuse, then diet until it became a way of life. Though you realize that this could mean hard, sometimes agonizing periods of self-reflection and personal honesty, you know that you will again find yourself on solid ground, but you leave this place already knowing that you are on the road to redemption.

Chapter 4

Cheese, Bacon, Eggs and Steak Do Not a Food Group Make

You can't get to heaven on a carb-free diet!

Why?

Let's Be Honest . . .

. . . 'cause you are always hungry, that's why! And, we all know that a hungry person is an angry person.

It's Saturday morning. You are on your highly anticipated, well-deserved vacation cruise. You slept in after your long, late night of carousing on the Lido deck of the beautiful ship. As you stare out at the incredible sight of blue waves stretched across the horizon, your mind drifts back to the events of the past twelve hours. The beautiful, calm expanse of ocean acts as a screen on which the movie of your life is being shown, and you shudder as you begin to replay each agonizing moment from the past evening.

Last night, you danced till your feet ached as you sipped your lukewarm tonic water with a sliver of lemon and pasted on your best game face. Why the game face? Well, it's because, while you delicately sipped your tepid, lukewarm (never was cold) tonic water with a sliver of lemon, you watched your family, your buddies, your lover, and your friends, down glass after glass and bottle after bottle of life-sustaining, fun-providing, idiot-producing, alcohol-laden CARBS. While you, you gracefully sipped on your glass of tasteless, tepid, lukewarm, never was cold tonic water with a sliver of lemon.

At the stroke of midnight, you watch as those evil, thoughtless, white-coated, tall-hatted, gorgeous providers of late-night cruise ship cuisine lay out the soul-robbing midnight spread. It was all piled high on tables covered with hot cheese pizza, cinnamon and raisin cookies, a rainbow of colors of ice cream and glass sculptures in the form of champagne bowls. You raise your eyes from your lustful (Deadly Sin 4) gaze at the delights that were scandalously set out before you and barely manage to escape being crushed as a frightening swarm of humanity rushes toward the tables, threatening to tilt the ship on its side. You swallow the anger (Deadly Sin 5) that washes over you when you think of all that you will be missing. With a forced smile you cover the envy (Deadly Sin 2) that surges through you as you observe the teeming crowds exhibiting inhuman acts of gluttony (Deadly Sin 3) in which you would gladly and shamelessly participate if only you had not decided to go on this Godforsaken starvation program.

As you watch this shameless display of wanton overindulgence and greed (Deadly Sin 6) you, my friend, stuff your agony deep down inside the empty spaces in your belly, right next to where a huge gas bubble is rumbling and threatening to kill you. You take a pass on the cheesecake and scrumptious finger sandwiches and ingest a few slices of unidentifiable cold cuts. The cold cuts are nestled up to a couple slices of off-color cheese and ten droopy-tailed cold shrimp without the wonderful cocktail sauce with its carb-filled ketchup. With downcast eyes and a heavy heart, you slowly make your way out of the dining hall and find a quiet corner where you can safely, gratefully, and noisily deal with the threatening eruptions from your nether regions without fear of exposure.

Finally, at 4 a.m., when everyone else sets out to bed, laughing and joking and patting their overstuffed bellies and overstuffed evening purses, bellies and purses stuffed full of glorious, wonderful carbs, you slink off to bed knowing you will face the recurring nightmare that has haunted you for almost three weeks. These terrifying dreams have surfaced every night for the past twenty-one days. These are the dreams in which the serving tray-sized plate, laden with the giant loaf of bread, the turkey-sized chicken drumsticks, the soup bowl-sized serving of potato salad, the maple syrup, cinnamon-covered slices of sweet potatoes, and luscious slices of bright red tomatoes chase you down the street followed by the largest knife and fork you have ever seen. You shake your head in complete despair and try to figure out what your excuse will be tonight when you crawl into bed and your darling wants to make shipboard memories for your later years. Some things just don't go well with an empty belly! As usual, the night passes with you in agony as hunger pangs threaten to break you in half. Then this morning, you crawled out of the tiny bunk with shaking knees and a stomach shrunken to your back and knew it would be bloated like a balloon by noon.

Your morning reverie is shattered as you sense a swarm of bodies rushing past you, and you know for sure that only food could cause otherwise rational people to act this way. Cruise ship breakfast is served, and you get caught up in the swarm. Now here you are at the breakfast buffet, and there they are. Yes, by God, there are those large, shiny, steaming trays that you have dreaded all night. You glance at the crisp, white card propped in front. What do you see? Is that your name neatly typed, in italics no less? You blink rapidly to clear your vision and, lo and behold, your name disappears and is replaced by the awful words, "*New Red Potatoes Smothered in Onions and Red Peppers.*" On and on it goes down the line, "*French Toast with Fresh Strawberries in Syrup,*" "*Fried Tamales with Jalapeños,*" "*Buttered Toast with Jelly."* Finally, you come to a tray with a label that makes your heart sing with joy, the one that truly has your name on it, *"Scrambled Eggs with Crispy Bacon."* You clutch your plate more securely, grab the shovel that passes for a serving spoon and lay open the treasure chest. And there it is. One lonely slice of over fried, two-hours-old bacon that none of the last twenty diners dared to choose. And just to the left of the last remaining sliver of antique pork rests the last spoonful of a cold, congealed substance that a few hours ago may actually have passed as scrambled eggs.

You pause, your spoon in midair, and you look around you. The room slowly comes into focus, and there they are, your heartless, unsympathetic, uncaring carbohydrate-consuming "frenemies" from last night, plates piled high with bread, potatoes, tamales, and breakfast burritos. Their faces are flushed with pleasure, their eyes glazed over with a kind of bliss you have not experienced in the twenty-one days since you sacrificed your life for that itty-bitty, teensy-weensy, yellow polka dot bikini that you couldn't fit into even when you were ten years old.

You hear the dual-channeled cacophony of the pounding in your chest and the pounding in your head, and you know the end has come. The anger (Deadly Sin 5) erupts in a frenzy of gluttony (Deadly Sin 3). The envy (Deadly Sin 2) that you have experienced over the past three weeks is subsumed by greed (Deadly Sin 6) as you charge blindly toward the carb-filled silver platters that you lusted over (Deadly Sin 4). Then you take pride (Deadly Sin 1) in the surge of power you feel as you march toward the life-supporting sustenance contained within those beautiful, gleaming silver containers.

As you make contact with the serving spoons neatly laid out for your use, you realize that with this newfound power, you will no longer have the need to consider breaking the sixth Thou Shalt Not (thou shalt not murder) over food you cannot eat. No longer will you steal cookies to hide in your purse, breaking Thou Shalt Not 8, and no longer will you be forced to give false testimony (Thou Shalt Not 9) about the grams of carbs you have consumed during the past day. Finally, no longer will you covet your neighbor's plate, sacrificing your soul to Thou Shalt Not 10. Why? Well, because at this precise moment, you realize with absolute certainty, that for you to get off this ship on your own two feet and not by going over the side then, thoughts of Thou Shalt Nots and Deadly Sins will have to be damned; you will eat, and the diet can go to hell!

As you reach into that first platter of mouth-watering smothered potatoes, waves of despair and self-loathing engulf you, and you recall the days and hours of cravings that you endured to get to this place and time. You wonder why. Why have I done this to myself? What led me to this place? You pause on this thought as the reality of your life surfaces. Slowly replacing the serving spoon on the saucer, you begin to see, feel, and know that it's all because you have really lost sight of the true you. It dawns on you that you no longer love yourself. It registers that you have missed the beautiful being you truly are, the fantastic, perfect being others see and whom you seem to have lost sight of. You sense the beginning of a struggle. This is a struggle to rediscover the person that, regardless of the external appearance, was made in the image and the likeness of the Creator and is, therefore, a perfect being. Now, with startling clarity, you remember some small voice from your early years reminding you of Jesus' commands to love God and to love thy neighbor as thyself. With shoulders squared and a smile a mile wide, you turn back to the food warming trays knowing what you have to do—that is, rediscover the true you.

As you sally up to your joyful friends with your plate containing one slice of French toast, one serving of red potatoes, one slice of ham, and a spoonful of veggies, your face breaks out into an illuminating smile, and you greet your friends. "Neighbors, I love you, and I love myself," and you know without a doubt that you are fulfilling Jesus' Commandments. You sigh a sigh of contentment as you silently acknowledge that you won't get to heaven on a carb-free diet, but you can certainly get there practicing moderation. For as Plato said, "Moderation, which consists in an indifference about little things, and in a prudent and well proportioned zeal about things of importance, can proceed from nothing but true knowledge, which has its foundation in self-acquaintance." I say, "To know yourself is to love yourself."

Chapter 5

The Twin Vices of Sex and Love – If It Feels Too Good to Be True, Then You Should Probably Quit

You can't get to heaven doing it with someone else's loved one!

Why?

Let's Be Honest . . .

. . . 'cause it's stealing when you try to write off the cheap motel bill as a corporate business expense.

It's Monday morning. You're on your way to work, and as usual these days, you are running behind. All you can think about is the fact that, recently, despite what seems to be your best effort, you are always late. Late, late, late. You try to remember the time when you were the first one in your office and the last to say goodnight to evening security and the cleanup crew. This morning, you make your way through traffic that seems to sense your mood and is moving like lumbering mammoths up a steep slope. Your mind wanders. You almost convince yourself that you caught a whiff of the awesome Jamaican Blue Mountain Roast you used to brew as soon as you walked into the office. You remember how the folks coming in late would sleepwalk toward the coffeepot. Where did those days go?

When did you lose your thrill, your drive, your desires, your ambitions, your zest for your job? You can't seem to remember when it all changed. Instead, these days you just seem to always be tired and late!

Images of your boss standing by the coffee pot glaring at you while surreptitiously glancing at his cheap watch float through your mind. You envision him calmly twirling that stupid little stick around and around in the awful tasting cup of coffee, the coffee you didn't get to make and won't get to enjoy because you are late. A feeling of panic overwhelms you as you remember the folder full of notes that you had so carefully placed on the kitchen counter last night, so you wouldn't forget it this morning. The folder was now still sitting just where you placed it. This morning, you knew for sure that all the angels had turned their backs on you at the same time when the blasted blow dryer that had been cranky for the past few weeks chose this particular day to finally give up the ghost and cease to blow.

Memories of the mad dash to get out of the house flash through your mind. As if your morning had not already started off in the pits of hell, the car keys you put in the side pocket of your purse last night managed to end up in your jacket pocket, the same jacket that somehow got lost under the sofa pillows and which took ten whole minutes to locate. Now, here you are, in a mad dash down the hall to your space in that place you have now come to so truly hate.

How do you know you hate it? Simple: that's one of the reasons you're always late. You collapse into your uncomfortable chair, knowing you need at least fifteen minutes to collect your thoughts before you can tackle the undoubtedly awful day that lay ahead. Unbidden, your mind floods with memories of the events of the weekend—events that brought you to this point today, late and miserable. You lower your eyes while rethinking the past forty-eight hours and gasp in horror as you realize, "Oh my God, I'm wearing the same pair of shoes I wore on Friday." Only today, the shoes are in two different colors, one black and one blue, just like the colors of your battered and bruised heart. From there, the day goes straight to the lowest level of hell.

What preceded this calamity? How did you ever get on this slippery slope to this living hell? How did you think your way into this mess that is your life? Then you realize, "That's it, that's the problem. I didn't think. I just did what I wanted because it felt so good!" You flash back to last Saturday evening to review your latest act of self-inflicted degradation and humiliation. Recounting the acts that caused your life to spiral out of control, you realize, after some contemplation, that your misery really did not start then. Truth be told, it started way before.

Actually, if you chose to be honest, you would have to admit that your fall from grace started over a year ago on a Monday morning so unlike this one, when the most beautiful male human being you had ever laid eyes on sauntered into your office. You instantly lost your soul. You remember clearly that when he introduced himself as the new assistant manager, you missed his name because of the clamor going on inside your head. What was that noise again? Oh, that's right, it was the sounds of Thou Shalt Not 3, crashing under the heels of your Jimmy Choos as you took the Lord's name in vain and silently mouthed the words, "Lordy, Lordy, Lordy, Sweet God Almighty. Tell me I've died and gone to heaven, and this is my just reward."

A feeling of embarrassment creeps across your cheeks as you recall the warmth that snaked its way up and over your thighs and stomach (Deadly Sin 4) when he turned, and you literally had to wipe the drool from your lips as he walked out of your office. Instantly, and with absolutely no doubt, you were willing to break Thou Shalt Nots 1, 2, 7, 8, 10, and even some that Moses himself was probably too scared to jot down on his supersized, stone Post-it Note. Now here you are: sad, late, and miserable.

Your mind drifts back to this past Saturday evening, almost a year after that first encounter. Your thoughts come to rest on the man who, over the past year, became the dream of your future, the delight of your life, the joy of your every moment. This man became the essence of your very soul, the holder of the keys to your happiness, the future father of your future phenomenal children, and the future partner of your golden years. It is then that you recall the sensation of a sinking feeling in the pit of your stomach when, on Saturday evening, after hours of waiting, you finally got the call to say that he couldn't see you this evening. In a hushed, whispering voice he explained that he couldn't see you because he had to go to dinner with the woman of his present, his wife, and their offspring. This was the woman whom you both only referred to as "she" or "her," and the fruit of "her" loins, whom you only knew as "they" or "them." You lost it then, your mind, that is.

Why? Why did you lose your mind? Was it because you didn't know about this woman presently in his life? Were you, by any chance, unaware of his dearly beloved offspring? Actually, no. That's not why you lost your mind and all sense of reason when he, once again, chose them over you. No way! It was just that the last time it happened, he told you it would never happen again except, of course, if it was somebody's birthday. It wouldn't happen again unless there was a real emergency like if *she* needed to get her hair done and *she* needed him to babysit, or if *her* parents were stopping by for an impromptu barbecue, or if, God forbid, the temperature rose above 80 degrees in Arizona on a Tuesday in the middle of a heat wave. These days, any excuse seemed to provide him with a reason to leave you alone, with nothing to keep you company but memories rehashed with eyes wide open, dreams and fantasies created in restless sleep, or a half-empty bottle of his favorite Pinot Noir.

It was this final act of abandonment that drove you to commit your first sin of last Saturday evening. That's what made you so angry (Deadly Sin 5). That's what made the waves of envy (Deadly Sin 2) roll over you like a tsunami. At that moment, an intense desire to break Thou Shalt Not 6 and commit acts of murder muscled its way into your heart and mind.

So what was his real excuse for not showing up to take you out to dinner at that cozy little diner hidden away and off the beaten track? The one with the lovely, quaint little motel conveniently tucked in under the swaying neon lights that flashed on and off, which he said reminded him of twinkling stars? The place he adored because of its seclusion and its quiet, sheltered ambience. You would never know.

Now here you were, stuck, wearing the little black dress that he told you to go ahead and buy as a gift, from him, and for which he said he would repay you but hadn't. You glance down at the four-inch heeled, fire-engine red stilettos that he fell in love with when you both spotted them in that little shoe boutique. He immediately offered to buy them for you. You remember how cute he looked when he reached for his wallet to pay for them and how embarrassed he was when he realized he didn't have his wallet with him. Nevertheless, he insisted that you purchase them, and as always, he promised to repay you. You shake your head in painful sadness when you finally admit that, as with so many other purchases, he still owed you for the dress, which you really didn't even like, and the blasted shoes which to be honest, now that you think about it, were too damn tight anyway. It is then that you realize that he even managed to convince you to charge the cheap hotel room on your credit card as a corporate business expense.

Even in the midst of your anger, a small smile crosses your lips as you picture the beautiful smoky grey pearls that he promised you for Christmas. Your smile turns to a frown as you recall that you saw *her* wearing a similar, perhaps even identical, set. You saw the pearls around *her* neck that evening when you ran into them coming out of a fancy uptown restaurant, the one that, according to him, *she* dragged him to, to meet with important friends of hers from out of town. You realize then that you still have not gotten your Christmas gift, which he told you he'd accidentally left at his mom's house and couldn't take back because she thought they were for her.

Sitting there in the dark on yet another lonely Saturday night, you feel confused, humiliated, and jealous. You begin to contemplate the ways in which you could get back to the safe, fictional place you had created in your mind. This was a place that you and your honey often talked about sharing, as soon as his children (ages five, three, and eight months) were out of college. Then you could both build a home together and reside in bliss. Thoughts of murder, (Thou Shalt Not 6), again flash across your mind, but you can't quite decide on just whom to inflict this madness, him, *her* or yourself. All you can think about as you wander around your living room, tears streaming down your face, is just how much you worship (Thou Shalt Not's 1 and 2) this wonderful, sexy, lying, cheating, gorgeous, scum bucket hunk of a man. Then the phone rings and as you make a mad dash to retrieve it, you break your pinkie toe on the leg of the coffee table—well, at least it felt like it was broken at the time.

You swore at the pain, limped to the sofa, retrieved the phone, and saw that the call was coming from the last person in the world you wanted to talk to at this moment. This was the one person who could gauge your body temperature, check your pulse, conduct a Breathalyzer test, read your moods from across town (or from another planet for that matter), and warn you of the moral dangers associated with Thou Shalt Nots 7, 8, and 10, all while asking you what you ate for dinner. It was Mom. As you wiped away your tears of pain, frustration, anger and humiliation, you chirped the cheeriest greeting humanly possible into the phone, "Hi Mom!" "So that fellow stood you up again, huh?" she responds. "I suppose he is working late again this evening? Didn't he work late the last two Saturday evenings also?"

But how did she know? Did everybody know? How foolish did you look to your friends and coworkers if they also knew? You stare at the phone in disbelief and look around the room to figure out where she is hiding; then you proceed to break Thou

Shalt Not 9 by calmly lying, "No Mom, he didn't stand me up. He had to visit his sick grandmother at the nursing home."

"Oh," chimes Mom, equally calmly, "you mean the grandmother that died a few months ago? You know, they really ought to consider burying those poor folks. Can't begin to imagine what it must smell like over there. But it's none of my business." There is a pregnant pause as she awaits a response from you that she knows is not forthcoming. Finally, she utters the words you know you can count on as she hangs up. "Bye baby. Remember, God loves you, and I do too."

That was really the last thing you remember before your trip past the bar to grab the bottle of Jose Cuervo that seemed to have become your constant companion and dearly beloved best friend over the past few months of lonely Saturday nights. As you fell into your empty bed, the bed that once cradled the passion that now seemed so far away, you wrapped your arms around yourself and tried to soothe your battered black and blue, and completely broken, heart. The tears streamed down your cheeks as you drifted off hoping to find some peace in your sleep tonight. As you drifted deeper into forgetfulness, you made a vow, a vow that tomorrow would be different. Tomorrow, you would begin to reclaim your heart and your soul. At least that was the last thing you remember until you woke up this morning, realized you had practically slept through the entire day on Sunday, and now had to go to that place that you used to love so much but now hated. Why? Because *he* was there.

Now you sit here, the past year flashing through your mind, like one would imagine the events of one's life flashing through the mind's eye just before death. In your mind's eye, you see and hear snippets of conversations long gone by. You remember the time your dearly beloved had convinced you, as you sobbed in his arms, that he didn't really love *her*. How gently he held you when he told you that you understood him so much better than *she* ever did and that they had not shared a bed or slept in the same bedroom since way before he met you. Now that you think about it, how did you miss the stark evidence presented by the eight-month-old? But no, wait, he explained that away as one of those situations in which *she* managed to manipulate him—that evil woman!

You feel the weight of it all as you slump at your desk and realize, for the first time, that you are doomed unless you awaken and search your soul for the reasons you allowed yourself to become caught in this snare of dishonesty and deceit. Resigned, you realize that you can in no way ascribe blame to this man. A rare moment of clear-headedness combined with a large dose of personal honesty allows you to reflect on your willing participation in a farce of great proportions. You look at your behavior and know that the only way out is to take your eyes off the man and look inward at yourself. How could you have become so complacent, so willing to accept so little love unless, of course, you had no love for yourself? How could you now begin the process of self-love that would save you from the seductive, scheming, illusive love of another woman's husband? For a moment, you feel lost. You have no answers, but then you pause. Suddenly, you have a moment of clarity. You hear your Mom's voice wafting gently through your mind, softly muttering the words she always uttered at every separation, "Baby, God loves you, and I do too." It was then that you knew, without a doubt, that you could start with someone on whose love you could always count.

You pick up the phone to make a few calls. The first goes to the late object of your desire—a desire now quickly fading. With a newly discovered realization of self-disgust and distaste and a heaping helping of personal honesty, you say quietly into the phone, "I am not available for dinner this Saturday, or any other." Then you pick up the phone once again and place another call. "Mama, how about dinner next Saturday night? Just you and me?"

The voice on the other end replies, "Baby, Mama's already got her little black dress on."

You look down at your feet, and with a smile on your lips, you say, “Wow, black and blue sure do look good on my pretty feet.”

Chapter 6

Sins of the Workplace: "Just Supplementing My Meager Paycheck"

You can't get to heaven stealing pens, paper clips, and toilet paper from the office or the snuggly bathrobe and toilet paper from the Hilton!

Why?

Let's Be Honest . . .

. . . 'cause the name monogrammed on your stolen hotel bathrobe won't match St. Peter's VIP check off list when you reach the pearly gates.

Actually, the same holds true of the little sample bottles of shampoo, lotion, mouthwash, and shower gel that we all rip off from the fancy, and not so fancy, hotel bathrooms. And how about the occasional towel set? Yes, I said set, as in towel, hand towel, and washcloth. Do we really think we can display them in the guest bathroom at home and not have everyone recognize them? Remember, we all have our own white "towel sets" too. And, some of ours are even monogrammed "*Hilton*" or "*Bellagio*" even though our last name is Jones.

Seriously folks, let's get back to the more grave issue of taking items, large or small, cheap or expensive, seemingly important or not, but items that do not belong to us. It all starts somewhere, and sooner or later, it leads to bigger things. Let's begin with the Post-it Notes and highlighters we need to edit our "work-related material" at home tonight. It's work related, right? So what could be so wrong with using work products at home? The answer to that could be something like this: "It's work-related," so why not take home your desktop computer along with the Post-it Notes, the staplers, the paper clips, the pens, and that extra ream of copy paper to be used with the printer you do not own.

While you're at it, why not just come in to work a little later and leave work a little earlier every day, so you can do all that "work-related" stuff at home? See the point? Where exactly are the boundary lines? We all know it begins with those small items for which we believe we can create perfectly rational justifications, and sooner or later, we end up trying to justify the "small" $10,000 short-term loan we took, without authorization, just to pay off Mom's medical bills.

Folks, there is a name for the action that led to taking home the first block of Post-it Notes or the first box of Bic pens. It is the same name we assign to taking that small, unauthorized, short-term loan—stealing—the action mandated against by Thou Shalt Not 8. Now, surely you remember the conversation you had with yourself the first time you broke this commandment. What did you say to yourself? "I'll bring it back tomorrow." Kinda difficult, wouldn't you say? This would be especially difficult if you stole it from the office and had already promised it to your dear little niece and nephew, Pookie and Boo, for their school supplies. Or what did you say when you stole the hotel towels? "Oh, I just need them to wrap these dirty shoes. Wouldn't want these dirty shoes to soil the beautiful monogrammed bathrobe I snatched also." What about the conversation that took place inside your head when you wrote and signed that first check, the one that didn't have your name on the bank account? You probably tried to convince yourself that you were not truly breaking the eighth Thou Shalt Not, which exhorts us against stealing. Because if you did try to convince yourself of that, then friend, you were *also* lying (Thou Shalt Not 9) to yourself, and it was simply the first of many lies yet to come.

Now, let us pause for a moment and ponder the reasons behind these thoughts and actions. What leads us to the place where access to another's property became a prerequisite for our own satisfaction and fulfillment? Let's begin with Thou Shalt Not 10, Thou shalt not covet. To covet is to desire that which belongs to another. No matter how we slice it, dice it, rationalize it, or try to justify it, when we take another's goods, it is because we want what isn't ours, be it from a friend, a family member, your office, Macy's or Wal-Mart. The bigger question, however, is: what is it that drives one to covet another's property? For the answer to that question, we must turn to the Seven Deadlies, where we can have our pick of any number of sins, mistakes, missed marks, or dastardly deeds waiting to be committed.

I want to reiterate a key point here. That is, when I use the word *sin* in this book, I am in no way attempting to lay on the sledgehammer of the "sins" of certain established belief systems. In these systems, if we are deemed to be serial committers of sins, we are bound to burn in a hell that is the making of some fire-breathing god or, at the very least, we will do time in the holding place called Purgatory. Instead, I want to remind you of the meaning of the word sin, which is to "miss the mark." So what mark are we missing with our choice of thoughts and actions? I suggest to you that the mark we are missing is the ability to look ourselves in the face and to see an honest person looking back. The mark we are missing is the ability to teach little Pookie and Boo the value of trust, self-worth, and integrity. The mark we are missing is the opportunity to go to sleep at night with a clean conscience, knowing that we have done unto others as we would have them do unto us.

Missing the mark is the envy (Deadly Sin 2) we exhibit while coveting (Thou Shalt Not 10) things that belong to another. It is the greed (Deadly Sin 6), that keeps us from being satisfied with what we have. It is the anger (Deadly Sin 5) we feel when we think others have what we want or deserve. It is the laziness, aka sloth (Deadly Sin 7) that binds us and perhaps keeps us from putting forth enough effort to work to buy what we need. The mark we are missing is our indulgence in pride, which is cautioned against by Deadly Sin 1, and which makes us take rather than ask for the things we think we need to have. Missing the mark is the hell we create and the heaven we avoid.

I believe desiring the possessions of others is perhaps one of the most common of all our follies, one that keeps us from living in our personal heaven and dooms us to a hell of our own creation. The idea of getting what we want, when we want it, regardless of the cost or the consequences, is one that many of us seem to have developed at an early stage in life, one that plagues us throughout our lives. This need to possess is so pervasive that we will even go so far as to obtain spectacular burial sites and overly decorated, gaudy boxes in which to make our final transition, all of which we purchase on a credit card since we can't afford to pay cash.

The good news is that this craving for material goods is a folly from which we can easily escape. Once we can get the notion through our minds that our behaviors are simply a reflection of a deep feeling of *lack* within our own being, then we can begin to find help in filling those empty inner spaces with attributes of far greater value. I am referring to attributes such as loving, sharing, and giving, which bring a much greater return than the trivial junk we choose to steal. Once we can reconcile ourselves to being personally honest, avoiding all deception and cover-ups, we begin to find that the joy obtained from loving, sharing, and giving will last a lifetime. We discover that the ink from that Bic is good only for a few lines, and the thrills from the last hotel towel will surely dissipate during the next hotel visit when the next opportunity for acquisition presents itself. Once our sense of personal honesty allows us to see this, we may start to ask the difficult questions: What about the love we are invariably searching for when we go on our quest for stuff? Where is the peace for which we are in constant pursuit? From where does this love and peace come? The first truth with which we need to reconcile ourselves is that love and peace DO NOT come from outside. They come from inside where God resides.

Unfortunately, most of us start our search on the outside before finding out that the stuff for which we have spent our lives searching is located right in our hearts and souls. The love of Christ, a "love that surpasseth knowledge" (Eph. 3:19) and the "peace of God which passeth all understanding" (Phil. 4:7), are ours free to have and to hold. We search for a God among idols and material goods, such as cars, homes, jewelry, and for some of us, even on the menu at a fine restaurant, when all we have to do is to look inside our own souls. According to Earnest Holmes, the founder of the Science of Mind philosophy, "*The only God man knows is the God of his own Inner life; he can know no other. This does not mean that man is God; it means that the only God that man knows is within, and the only life man has is from within. This is why Jesus said that the Kingdom of heaven is within and why He prayed: 'Our Father which art in heaven'.*" p. 343. It is also Jesus who preached that all that we needed in order to find love and peace was contained in the two Commandments: To love God and to love our neighbor as ourselves—this, and only this, would guarantee us a clear path back to our own personal heaven.

Along this path back to our personal heaven, we can begin the fulfilling and immensely rewarding act of giving rather than taking. Begin to think of the things that should really matter the most as we pass along this journey we call life. In the end, we take nothing with us, so do we really need to hoard so much now? If you lost it all tomorrow, as so many around us have done, are we any less for that loss? Perhaps we should start to look around us and think of how much less we can live with rather than how much more we can't live without. Ridding ourselves of material worth and exposing our self worth will invariably force us to become intimate with the practice of personal honesty.

You will soon discover that the immense value of a life built on a foundation of personal honesty far outweighs a closet full of mass produced hotel towels, Post-it Notes, bathrobes or paper clips. After all folks, how many pens do we really need?

Chapter 7

It's Mine 'Cause I Paid for It

You can't get to heaven wearing someone else's hair, someone else's nails, a Victoria secret push-up bra and claim it's all yours 'cause you paid for it!

Why?

Let's Be Honest . . .

. . . 'cause tonight you have to take them all off and look in the mirror, that's why!

Hell-o ho-ney, come in, come in. Vat you vant today? Mani? Pedi? Pic u colla ho-ney, pic u colla. Sit hea, sit hea. We tek good kea you ho-ney. Vat u name? My name Susy. I tek good kea you ho-ney."

It's that time again. Saturday morning, and all is well in your neighborhood nail salon. There you are, unvarnished acrylics exposed for all the world to see, and nails you haven't seen in six years peek out from beneath concrete-like imitation talons that look like they belong to a T. rex. Forty-five minutes later, bathed in the essence of Eau de Acetone No. 5, you emerge from China Jade Salon where your nails are your nails, "cause you paid for 'em."

Then it's off to ***Shake, Shimmer & Shine Salon*** where, for the next few torturous hours, you will sit patiently while some gum-popping, stiletto-wearing, overly painted artiste will sew, weave, stitch or glue something nylon, polyester, animal, or human to your head and call it your hair, and it will become yours "cause you paid for it."

Finally, you find yourself, near exhaustion, your feet aching, your back throbbing, your nail beds screaming from the effects of the whirring drill bit that Jung Soon (aka Susy) ran over them time and time again all the while attempting to put out the threatening flames with the pad of her thumb and blowing cool puffs of breath while gently muttering, "I so sorry ho-ney, so sorry. Al-mos fini." However, you don't pause for a moment except to hoist your bag containing at least one week's salary or some badly abused credit cards higher up on your shoulder. A look of steely determination is painted in a fierce line across your knitted brow. Exhaustion and pain? "Be gone!" You charge forward. The quest for perfection is by no means over.

You pause for a moment to search through the mobile home that passes for a purse, and for a few harrowing moments, a feeling of panic rises in your throat as you frantically search for, and then mercifully retrieve, the Post-it Note with your makeover list for today. You glance up and spot the next stop on your way to finding the perfect item designed to make you feel fulfilled and fabulous and real, and the charge continues. Just what every woman needs, her Victoria Secret buy one, get one free, push-up, move over, shape-shifting, up-thrusting, blizzard-resistant, over-the-shoulder, under the arm, underwater flotation device, "***Natural"*** bra in black and beige with the matching booty-creating or restraining panties.

Two hours later, as you drag yourself out of the store, blissfully clutching your beautiful shopping bag filled with shimmering, glimmering, ecstasy-guaranteeing items, you know for sure that underneath that nearly topless dress that you bought for the party tonight, you will have the best looking pair of knockers in the room. How do you know? Simple. Because you bought and paid for them, and that makes them yours.

Fluttering those fabulous silken, individually applied eyelashes you smile charmingly at your dinner companion, confidently exposing your expensive, lily-white veneers. You know you are being admired for your stunning looks. Why? Because you bought and paid for your looks, and "that makes them yours." Finally, as the long evening draws to a close you begin your journey home, smiling with sheer satisfaction at the impression you made on the crowd tonight. You remember the pleasure you felt at the audacious, unveiled admiration in the eyes of men and women alike as they openly ogled you from head to toe. The fabulous hair, the fanning eyelashes, the beautiful blue of your brown eyes, your plump lips, your luscious chest, your tightly held stomach and firm buttocks, the pearly nails and your well-groomed cuticles. Your body practically quivers with joy and satisfaction as you enter your bedroom and begin your ritual in preparation for a night of rest and peaceful, honest reflection.

The transformation begins as you start the slow process of removing the pieces of your public self. Bit by bit, you take off the mask until finally, the true, real, less than perfect you emerges. There you stand, naked for only your eyes to behold, and what do you see? What you see tonight is a slow descent into your own personal, private hell.

As you look into the full-length mirror that provides the pathway to your mental and emotional demise, you realize that you are staring into the mirror of your own soul. It is there that you see the Deadly Sins of pride and envy (Deadly Sin 1 and 2) that caused you to begin the transformation into someone you now hardly recognize. You slowly come to terms with how callously you broke Thou Shalt Not 9 with the lies you perpetrated to become an image that your very own mother would not recognize.

You note the seething anger (Deadly Sin 5) that makes you dislike your own hair, lips, bosom, and even the eyelashes that guard and protect your beautiful brown eyes. Your breath almost leaves your body from the pain you feel when you remember how sweetly you smiled earlier tonight when your dinner companion admired your beautiful baby blue eyes and your perfect teeth. Cringing with mortification, you recall how effortlessly you broke Thou Shalt Nots 5 and 9 regarding dishonoring your parents by falsely attributing your soft, plastic, dye-created eye color and beautiful, synthetic enamel teeth to good genes.

Continuing to stare at the reflection of the image you manufactured, you slowly peel away the mask and finally reveal the real, true, beautiful you. You then take the first step that will lead you back from the edge of the hell you now realize is of your own creation. In despair, you ask yourself the ultimate question, "Who am I?" Then the questions come tumbling out in rapid succession. "Why am I so unhappy with the true me, that I have to completely disguise myself to like myself?" "What has led me to dislike myself so much that I had to create a new me?" Hopefully, you get to the toughest, but most important questions, "How do I find my way back? How do I begin the process of loving myself again?"

The answer is that the only way to begin the process is through the path of personal honesty. You should know that the keys to opening the door to your personal heaven are in your hands, and the desire to take the first step in is already there. This became evident when you looked into that mirror, saw your own soul, and realized you did not like what you saw reflected. Your next challenge comes in making the effort and finding the strength to take the next steps toward getting help, internally or externally, to move yourself back onto the path toward your own personal heaven.

So tonight, as you wash away the blush that stains your cheeks and remove the glimmering colors of the rainbow from your eyelids, you ponder the state of your life and pause in deep contemplation. Next comes the arduous task of removing the eyeliner, lines so artfully drawn as to produce almond-shaped eyes that could almost allow you to pass for an Asian in the dark. With the cleansing away of each carefully applied layer, you expose the real you, and tonight something strange happens. You realize that you can almost manage to look at the face in the mirror, something you have not done for a very long time. Perhaps there can be a true sense of peace somewhere within your own being, and maybe this place can be your heaven. It is here, in your personal heaven, that you will experience a realization that you are indeed a beautiful person, a person who is powerful enough, astute enough and confident enough to realize that beauty really is in the eyes of the beholder, and that you are the only beholder to whom you need to cater.

With time, patience, and an increased level of awareness, you will come to know that you are made in the likeness and the image of your Creator, and you will recognize that this Creator is sheer perfection, and therefore so are you. Eventually, you will acknowledge that the only thing you need to do to be perfect is to learn to love yourself as you truly are. You do that by loving the perfect God that resides in you, and then you can begin the task of loving others around you. You love them by being honest with them as you become personally honest, honest enough to trust them to see and to love who you truly are.

Through your reflection in the mirror, you believe you see a glimmer of light peek out from within you. It is a light you can hardly remember seeing; it has been so long. You pray that this inner light will illuminate the path that you can take out of the darkness into a healthy, clear, uncompromising relationship with the real you. This light helps you to see that in order to retrieve the real you, you must conquer, master, and destroy the false you. As you wipe away the last remaining residue of that image, you find yourself humming that tune your grandmother taught you so very long ago. It was a song from a much sweeter time, a time when you were a much simpler and more beautiful you. And so you hum . . .

♪♫This little light of mine, I'm gonna let it shine, ♪♫

♪♫ ♪Oh, this little light of mine, I'm gonna let it shine. ♪♫ ♪

♪♫ ♪This little light of mine, I'm gonna let it shine, ♪♫

♪♫ ♪Let it shine, let it shine, let it shine.♪♫

Chapter 8

What's The Rush? That Left Turn At Albuquerque Might Just Land You In The Desert.

You can't get to heaven taking the shortcut!

Why?

Let's Be Honest . . .

. . . 'cause you just might end up in a ditch, that's why!

How many times a day do you set out to tackle a task, large or small, and your immediate thought goes something like this—*Now, what is the easiest, fastest way to do this?*—rather than *Now, what is the best, most efficient way to get this done?* Many of us may actually need to reread both of these questions to get a grasp of the subtle, yet critical, difference between the two. Once we have examined them closely, however, we can easily recognize that one looks for a way out, while the other looks for a way through.

The first question reflects the current prevailing mentality with which many of us approach our lives. We are forever in a rush to get through one task or one life event, so we can get on to the next experience. What we seem to be missing, in our haste, is how much we are losing out on many of the vital details and subtleties inherent in our tasks.

It starts early and grows more frantic with each passing day. Let's take the example of childbearing and childrearing. Once upon a time, we sat back and waited for Mother Nature and Father Time to get together and make a love connection and provide us with a little concoction, that sooner or later (generally nine months later) turned into Little Jimmy or Little Jane. For many of us now, though, we simply cannot wait while Mother Nature and Father Time synchronize their PDAs. Instead, armed with a checkbook in one hand and a turkey baster in the other, we march off to the nearest baby depot for a quick pickup.

Now, for many a patient couple or even a single individual, nature may have already determined that this high-tech method, for which we thank the god of technology, is indeed the only route to our destination—blissful parenthood. For those folks, we say, "Have a safe, blessed and fruitful journey." For many others, however, this high-tech route has become a shortcut. These folks would be the ones among us who say, "I don't have the time to waste looking for Mr. or Mrs. Right. I want Little Jimmy or Little Jane right now." This statement is often preceded or followed by one that goes something like this, "All my friends my age and with my education and income already have their own Little Jimmy or Jane; why shouldn't I?"

Well folks, it is at this point where we commit the first of our infractions, envy, as in (Deadly Sin 2) or Thou Shalt Not 10, which admonishes against coveting your neighbor's house, his wife, his ass, or his sperm or her eggs. Of course, any violation of these rules invariably results in many more slips and slides away from the highway to heaven's pearly gates and down the shortcut that is the back alley to hell on earth.

Naturally, once you have speed-dated your way to parenthood with that test tube and claimed your prize at the door, other infractions could follow. These could include the innumerable times during which you will misuse the Lord's name, Thou Shalt

Not 3, on those countless nights when, mateless, you will walk the floor of the nursery, wishing you had someone to take second shift of the "midnight miseries."

Think about the obvious lying (Thou Shalt Not 9) you will do when in an inevitable state of mind-numbing sleep deprivation, you say to Little Jimmy or Little Jane, "I swear to God, I wish I had left you safely swimming around in your cozy little test tube," all while knowing full well you don't mean it. Imagine if you had waited for Mr. or Mrs. Right. You might just have had a real, grownup, human person on whom to unload your misery—and the precious bundle.

Then, on Saturday or Sunday morning you arise, bleary-eyed and half stupid from exhaustion and go to the office, committing Thou Shalt Not 4. Why the weekend work? Well, because, in your blissless, single-parent, dog-tired state, you had to go in late and leave early on many a day. So now, you have to make up all those extra hours, so you can afford to buy all the diapers, formula, and designer wear you need for Little Jimmy or Janey.

If we were to ever allow ourselves to pause for a moment of personal honesty in order to question the true motives behind our incredible decision to bring another being into existence, especially under these circumstances, what would our true answers be? Would it be a certain level of pride (Deadly Sin 1) in our presumed genetic superiority, which creates in us the desire to duplicate or to re-create our own being? Would it be our desire to have something that others have, Thou Shalt Not 10 and Deadly Sin 2? Would it be our overwhelming need for one more trophy, Thou Shalt Not 2? Or could it be a need to fill our empty inner spaces by getting more and more and more (Deadly Sin 6)? What drives some of us to take some of the shortcuts that we take? Perhaps we should all ask ourselves that question as we drive to the office to redo yet another botched assignment, botched because of the shortcut we took in the first place.

Speaking of the office: Honestly, what of the shortcuts we take just to get through our day, or our job, without ever thinking of the consequences of our actions? Let's pause for a moment to ponder some of the many unrecognized areas of our lives through which we take shortcuts rather than endure the longer, but more rewarding, journey. We take a shortcut with diet pills rather than exercising to lose the weight that we gained by taking a shortcut through the fast-food drive-through. We take the shortcut through the drive-through rather than stopping at the grocery store to shop for the healthy meal we could cook at home. Out of sheer laziness (Deadly Sin 7) (aka I don't have the time), we take the shortcut and microwave the frozen meal rather than take the time to slice and dice and cook, and we ruin our health with all of the above. We ladies take a shortcut when we get acrylics and tips because we can't wait while our own healthy nails grow in.

Men and women alike, we take shortcuts and invest in ten pieces of property in hopes of getting rich quickly rather than guaranteeing our family's security with one paid-for home. Then we lose it all when other bigger investors take their own illicit shortcuts, and they lose it all for us. We encourage our children to take shortcuts by using calculators; then we groan in despair when they can't make change for a dollar. Not to worry though, who uses a dollar anymore when we can take a shortcut and use our debit cards and credit cards? Then we do away with the tedious chore of balancing and maintaining our finances while someone or something at the bank does it for us. After all, the government can take a shortcut and bail out the banks when we overextend ourselves and can't pay our bills. Of course, we all soon come to painfully realize that these shortcuts eventually leave us in a ditch!

We take shortcuts in our relationships. We meet through e-romance or speed dating. We have a relationship through abbreviated e-mails and text messages, "I ♥ U." We break up using more text messages, "I H8 U." Whatever happened to the days of long summer romances that culminated in early spring weddings and forever loves? Now we seem to enjoy meeting at breakfast, indulging in a romance and wedding through lunch, and divorcing over dinner.

At our jobs, we have all become experts at taking shortcuts. We have lost touch with the desire or the drive for perfection in our work, and replaced it with a quest for quantity (Deadly Sin 6). We clamor for more sales, more clients, more revenue, taking less and less time and using less and less effort *attempting* to provide more and more quality. Many times, if we were to stop and evaluate our motives, with an eye to personal honesty, we would recognize that we do all of this just to guarantee that we outdo our friends and colleagues (Deadly Sin 5, Thou Shalt Not 10), but with as little effort as possible (Deadly Sin 7).

We speed raise our children in a quest for greatness, so they can keep up with Mary Sue's kids, while teaching them to commit Deadly Sins 2, 6, and break Thou Shalt Not 10. No longer do our children play baseball one season, football in another, and then take the summer off to just be kids. Why waste time being a kid when they can take the shortcut to greatness with hockey, soccer, tennis, and guitar lessons, and all in one afternoon?

Why the rat race? Why the speed? Why the shortcuts? Why have we lost touch with the desire to do it right in our drive to do it quickly? For what are we searching? What do we expect to achieve? What is it that generally drives us down the back alleys of life? What are we chasing? Could it simply be that we have all just grown lazy?

Well, if we were to slow down for a moment of personal honesty, many of us would soon realize that in our quest for more and more externals, we have developed and ignored a growing internal emptiness. Our gluttony, our greed, our envy, our pride, our covetousness have led us to a place where we can never be truly satisfied. We seem to constantly lust for more, be it people or things. We are willing to cheat, steal, and even kill, to get what we want quickly. Then we disintegrate into fits of anger when we recognize that we are still empty and unfilled and that we still want more. Our anger and resentment multiply when we see others around us increase their holdings, and we redouble our efforts and take more shortcuts just to keep up with the Joneses, the Trumps, the Kardashians, or whoever becomes the latest object of our admiration. In all of this mad rush, we seem to have lost touch with who we truly are as individuals. We no longer find joy in being ourselves as we desperately seek to be someone else. We no longer find pleasure in our achievements as we seek to do more, own more, and make more than the person next door.

Moving at break-neck speed and working to develop and use our shortcuts, we fail to recognize that by standing still for a moment and taking stock of our own lives, rather than the lives of others, there might actually be something to be happy about. We could discover that the slower, more thoughtful, reasonable journey may be what we need to fill our empty spaces. Perhaps we should dust off the old admonition to "stop and smell the roses." Slow down and take the time to enjoy the scenery of life. Look at and speak to the people we meet on our daily commute through this existence. Invariably, shortcuts take us down the terrifying, uncertain back alleys and back roads of life. On the other hand, the open roads and beautiful vistas of the slower, truer path through life often bring us to our true destinations, relaxed and fulfilled. No telling who we may meet and what experiences we will have as we move slowly and steadily along the way. Perhaps we could consider skipping the next text message or email and make a real phone call, "Let's have a long, slow lunch and catch up."

Chapter 9

Children: No, Not My Little Angels!

You can't get to heaven if you raise your monsters to terrorize other folks and make them lose their souls!

Why?

Let's Be Honest . . .

. . . 'cause ladies and gentlemen, monsters are monsters, even if they are your precious little monsters.

"Child, you gonna make me lose my soul up in here. Get yo' narrow behind in this house right now 'fore I kill you!" "Darling, Mommy's nerves are just a little frazzled right now. I'm about to count to three before I put you in timeout. See who'll be sorry then!"

Surely, you have heard one of the above remarks, or a variation on the theme, depending on your heritage, if you know what I mean. Those are the words of a desperate parent on the verge of a nervous meltdown, or they could be the warning being issued to an offspring just before Thou Shalt Not 6 (Thou shalt not commit murder) gets blasted into smithereens and a one-way trip to the penitentiary ensues.

Yes, moms and dads, those little people who once warmed the cockles of our hearts with their cooing and spitting and toothless smiles can sometimes grow into little beings that sprout horns and fangs while we are out for an evening of fun and relaxation. While we have our backs turned, taking the mouthwatering chocolate chip cookies that we just made for our little overweight darlings out of the oven, these once adorable, helpless creatures can mutate into little gremlins.

Where did these little monsters come from? you ask yourself. *What happened to the angels I produced not so long ago? When did they turn into perfect replicas of their father's parents—just shorter? How can I get rid of them without anyone noticing?* Well, you can't. You created them; you deserve to live with them! "Me?" You are perhaps shrieking at this precise moment. Well, I'm not your child, and don't you dare yell at me. Yes, I said, you!

You see, folks, this is precisely how it starts. It begins with a yell here or there during a moment of frustration. It begins with a "yes" that should be a "no" during an instance of weakness. It begins with no response during a period when careful attention should be shown. On and on it goes until one day, when we aren't looking, they morph into creatures we no longer recognize, and we can hold no one responsible but ourselves. Lack of attention and lack of care on behalf of our most precious resource, our children, are perhaps the greatest sins we can commit. Remember that to sin means to "miss the mark," and unfortunately, many of us are missing the mark when it comes to raising our children—the replacements we created to carry on God's work on this planet.

When our children miss the mark, we have no one to hold responsible but ourselves—not the teachers in the classroom, not the ministers in the churches, not the guidance counselors in the school office, not the grandparents, not the friends or neighbors. It has always been my firm belief that children are the rent we pay for the privilege of being on this planet—I suspect that's why it's called parenting (*pay*-renting). A huge part of this rent is paid by taking responsibility for their care, nurturance, and well-being. That care, nurturance, and well-being includes their mental, physical, and spiritual health—and is not covered by the latest in designer wear or gear.

So when and where did this sad act of missing the mark with our precious charges start? Well, if we are willing to spend some time pondering this question with *personal honesty* as the guide post, I imagine we will find that it started when we broke Thou Shalt Nots 1 and 2 right after their birth. How long was it before we decided this child was so special, we couldn't even find time to pray because we had to spend so much time changing and re-changing the little idols into the new designer outfits we couldn't afford and they didn't need? This was all so that our girlfriends and neighbors could see how proud (Deadly Sin 1) we were of little Bratella or little Demonel and how much money we spent on the little idol we worship (Thou Shalt Nots 1 and 2).

Next to go? Thou Shalt Nots 3, 6 and several of the Deadly Sins as we go through our next few years exclaiming to everyone who will listen or pretend to listen to us, "Oh my God, isn't my baby just beautiful? Everybody, just look at my Little Boo's eyelashes, look how much hair Baby Boo has. Oh God, I just worship my Baby Boo. I would just die if anything happened to my Boo. Look at those long fingers. With fingers like that, I am just going to have to rob a bank to pay for the piano lessons. You know I would just kill anyone who tried to come near my Baby Boo!"

Later, when Mom and Dad, ours that is, come to visit and dare to suggest that we get out and get some air or some color, since we have started to turn ashy or green from lack of exposure, we immediately destroy Thou Shalt Not 5 and Deadly Sin 5 by rudely and angrily pointing out that they are "old school" and that they don't know a thing about raising babies in this technological age. After all, who needs advice from the same people who can't figure out how to open the last sixty or so emails with the last 900 photos we sent to the rest of the family? Obviously, they don't care about this new little miracle and can, therefore, keep their opinions and advice to themselves.

Our new, and now seemingly habitual, line of thought appears to contain some threat to break Thou Shalt Not 6 and commit murder, as we contemplate what we would do if someone dared to look cross-eyed at our precious offspring. The threat to break this particular Thou Shalt Not seems to stay on our mind and is generally focused on the outside world. That is, until the day we have completed the destruction of said offspring with questionable parenting techniques, at which time the threat to break this Thou Shalt Not is now directed at said offspring.

In the meantime, however, we are certainly not above breaking Thou Shalt Not 8, if necessary, to provide our children with whatsoever he or she may ask for lest they have a temper tantrum in public. A temper tantrum, of course, would force us to break Thou Shalt Not 9 as we lie about the fit the demonic child is having and blame the ruckus on a nonexistent stomachache which we claim was caused by the little darling eating too many veggies at lunch; yeah right! Or we may even be pushed into resorting to the ever faithful, much-abused standby, "Oh, the poor baby is just so tired. He missed his nap today; poor baby." Well, I can only guess that poor baby has been missing several other nap times during these growing years as we watch the behavior go from bad to worse, and the baby tantrums turn into shotgun-toting teenage fits of rage.

By the way, this is where we contribute to other people around us missing the mark when they break Thou Shalt Not 3 and take the Lord's name in vain. "Dear Sweet Lord, give me five minutes in a closet with that child or her mother, and I bet that little demon spawn will never have another temper tantrum," all the while breaking Thou Shalt Not 9 and lying "Oh, honey, don't feel bad, don't worry about it, my little babies did the same thing 'til they were 22."

These types of unacceptable behaviors have become so typical in our darling children these days, that we even have names for them. Even now we refuse to be honest with ourselves and blame it on the true source. Rather than call it Mommy's and Daddy's *"terrible failure to take charge of this poor two year old,"* we blame the age and call it the "*terrible twos,*" as if this magic number actually had something to do with why dear Pookie or Boo turned into a monster. No folks, personal honesty time. The terrible twos were brought about by us as terrible parents MISSING THE MARK and failing in our responsibilities. I suggest that since we are the ones who are missing the mark as far as our two-year-old children are concerned, we should be the ones that pay the penalty for the actions they engage in at eighteen or twenty!

So what is the answer to our current dilemma? I suggest that we take the time and make the effort to lovingly but firmly discipline our dearly beloved children early and reap the benefits early. Time, love, and tenderness are what it takes—I do believe it is as simple as that—not time on the computer or with the latest video game or shopping for the latest gizmo to keep them busy and out of our hair, but time with our greatest investment, our children. It is what we owe the planet. It is what we owe ourselves. It is the rent we owe to God. Honestly, don't you want to pay up?

If we are commanded to love our neighbor, is it not reasonable to assume that we are to love our children? To love our children requires that we evaluate ourselves in an honest, forthright, albeit painful manner. Where are we dropping the ball? Yes, we are busy, but yes, we knowingly and consciously took on the added responsibilities at the office. For some, these added responsibilities are a matter of necessity, necessary to the care and nurturing of the offspring.

For far too many of us, however, our added responsibilities serve only to edify ourselves and to raise our stature in the eyes of the world. Where will those admiring folks be when our lives fall apart because of the actions of a wayward child? Will they say, "Oh yes, Mom, yes Dad, we heard that dear sweet Jeffery is in the slammer, but look how well you made those numbers at the office last week! Just look at the fabulous home he will have to come home to when they let him out in twenty-five years. So don't worry, Mom and Dad, it will all come out in the wash." Well, the only wash here will be our dirty laundry that is going to be hung out on the neighborhood gossip fence or the evening news for all to see. Loving our children means protecting them from the world, its influences, and sometimes even from our own pride, envy, greed, anger, etc. It may even mean sacrificing some of our own wants and needs.

So folks, let us take a time out for a moment of personal honesty. For those of us already into the task of raising our precious charges, perhaps we can pause and consider if, how, and where we are dropping the ball with our parenting responsibilities. Are we truly *there* through the easy times and the tough times? Are we using work or play as a means of avoiding the difficult challenge of being present for the raising of our children? Are we willing to make a sacrifice to complete this task? What are we willing to sacrifice?

For those of us who are just now contemplating this awesome undertaking, perhaps a large dose of personal honesty is even more crucial. You know the old truism, "you can't put the toothpaste back into the tube." So why not take a really long moment and ask ourselves "why?" Is it for all the right reasons? Is your reason for procreating a truly selfless one, like having the desire to create and prepare good stewards for our planet? Or, is it just a vain desire to create an extension of yourself? In that case, does the world really need another you or is one enough? Only you can determine the true answer to any of these questions. However, answer them you must, so that you can be successful in the sometimes toughest, but always most rewarding, job of your life, pay-renting.

Chapter 10

Family: Can't Live with Them, but You Can't Kill 'Em.

You can't get to heaven if you knock off a loved one!

Why?

Let's Be Honest . . .

. . . 'cause they won't let you in, even with a justifiable homicide pass.

There are two types of families. First, there is the family that acquires you. Necessarily included in this group of folks would be your mom and dad, your stepmom and stepdad, your adopted mom and dad, your foster mom and dad, and all the current variations on the theme. Then there is the family that you acquire. This group of folks may include your mother-in-law and father-in-law, stepmother-in-law and stepfather-in-law, or your adopted mother-in-law—well, you get the point. Like it or not, these are just the plain facts of life. There does, however, seem to be another fact of life regarding families. That is, regardless of how we come by them, once you have moved away from your familial home and set up our own domicile, these people gain a shelf life of about the same duration as fish and cooked cabbage—about three days.

Yes, yes, I know, we all just love and adore our dear moms and pops. Despite this, we also know that it is so much easier to love them from afar. Things just seem to mellow out once we have left their home and we no longer need them for *our* guidance and sustenance or for *their* checkbook. Somehow, once that bond is severed, even if only superficially, we start to experience strange, and often unpleasant, thoughts about ever sharing the same space with them again. All of a sudden, they take on the menacing countenance of things prowling in the dark and going bump in the night, things to be avoided at all costs.

Sound, rational, reasonable, and reliable research (aka soap operas), those enduring bastions of true family life and relationships, seems to indicate that the further removed these people are from us by blood, that is, those of the *in-law* variety, the more menacing they are. The more menacing they are, the more determined they are to cause us to run into those obstacles (Deadly Sins and Thou Shalt Nots), which could conceivably keep us out of heaven and even guarantee us a one-way ticket into hell.

First, let us start with the particular species of family generally referred to as "his (blankity blank) mother" or "my (blankity blank) mother-in-law." The "blankity blanks," when actually verbalized, generally break 'Thou Shalt Not 3' related to misusing the name of the Lord your God. This is the woman who gave birth to the love of your life, a love which you could not possibly conceive of living without. This is the progenitor of your dearly beloved whose love and kindness know no bounds. This is the same woman who often exhibits sheer terror-inducing, gut-wrenching, undercover meanness.

Why undercover? Because this meanness often manifests in the form of signs and signals and generally inaudible vocal frequencies and horrific facial distortions that no one else seems to be capable of seeing or hearing but you and the dog. For example, this morning, you crawled out of your sickbed to make her son a hot breakfast before he left for work. It seemed impossible to you that her son managed to miss the ugliness on her face as she peered at the eggs cooking in the skillet. How could he not have seen the look of disgust on her wrinkly face after she sneaked the slice of bacon from the napkin where it lay draining? Furthermore, what about the clucking of her tongue against her loose dentures and the tick of her over-plucked, raised eyebrows as she pretended to scrape imaginary burn from the toast? All you know is that the minute he kissed your cheek, thanked you for a wonderful breakfast and went to brush his teeth, the dear woman, sotto voce, claimed that she could tell that the coffee wasn't hot enough, the eggs were overdone and the toast was burnt, all by the look on her "poor baby boy's" puckered-up face.

As the anger (Deadly Sin 5) washed over you, you curled your lips and prepared a tart response and paused in mid retort. It was then that you remembered your promise to yourself to fiercely guard against ever committing Thou Shalt Not 5, that is, dishonoring your mother and your father. You swallow hard and seal your lips. You seal your lips only long enough for you to realize that she really wasn't your mother after all, and the Thou Shalt Nots didn't say anything about mothers-in-law. You let her have it then, both barrels, sotto voce, just before you scurried off back to bed where you should have stayed in the first place, terrified puppy in tow.

You lay in bed for hours, tossing and turning, as you recalled the many times you gently, and not so gently, tried to explain to your darling just how evil (well *unkind,* was the word you generally used) his mother could be. It occurs to you that never, not even once, had he ever acknowledged this side of the "saint" who was his dear mom. His brothers' wives had all seen the less than saintly side of her, but his brothers were never able to support their wives either. Not dear old mom! Finally, you gave up and went the way of the other sisters-in-law and just stopped trying to be honest about the old bat. Anything for a peaceful life, even a few little white lies.

It was almost noon when your dearly beloved called from work to check on you and to find out if dear mom was taking good care of you. Without thought, you broke Thou Shalt Not 9, by lying to him that dear mom couldn't be treating you any better than if she were your very own mother. As you blow him good-bye kisses through the phone, you hear the first grumble in the pit of your stomach, and you realize how hungry you are. After all, when you got angry this morning you scraped the last two perfectly good slices of breakfast toast into the trash can. Now here it is, noontime, and not a bite, and there she is sitting in front of the television. You know because you can hear the sounds of *As the World Turns* emanating from the living room.

As thoughts of murder and mayhem (Thou Shalt Not 6) course through your mind, you drag your aching body from your room and begin to forage through the refrigerator. You are so ravenous that you can hardly contain the pangs of greed and gluttony (Deadly Sins 3 and 6) that overwhelm you as you pile the food on the table. You are thirty-eight hundred calories into comfort food, and you have almost successfully managed to squelch the guilt that rears its ugly head in response to your assault on Deadly Sins 3 and 6. Then it, the guilt that is, rears its head again, and you suddenly pause in mid-gulp as you realize what this could mean in the next day or two when you begin to recover. You recall all the pride (Deadly Sin 1) it took to keep that twenty-six inch waistline, and you immediately begin to regret what you have done to your ailing body. Then you spy the light at the end of the tunnel as you realize that, wait, guilt is not a sin; it's just a self-inflicted wound with which you can live, and your spirits soar again with the next forkful.

As you crawl away from the table, you stop and think that perhaps, just perhaps, you should have taken the time to offer the evil one something to eat. Just then waves of drowsiness float over you, and you barely make it back to bed, acknowledging that now you know exactly how a sloth feels (Deadly Sin 7). You are climbing into bed when you hear the channel change and the seemingly interminable introductory melody of *All My Children* comes wafting through the halls into your bedroom. You feel the tiny hairs rise on the back of your scalp. You notice the tightening of your brows and the clenching of your jaw that you know are guaranteed to age your face by ten years over the next ten minutes. The thought enters your mind then that unless you do something to change the way you feel about the "*unkind*" one, you will certainly run the risk of breaking some more of the over 700 Thou Shalt Nots that Moses was too exhausted to write down, or committing some Deadly Sin that has not yet been invented.

As you drift in and out of sleep, you hear the sound of your beloved's car pulling into the driveway and you hear that other voice. It is dear mom singing out to you, loudly enough for all the neighbors in the next ten towns to hear. "Sweetie, can I get you something to eat? I know you must be starved." Just as your beloved enters the door, you hear yourself reply, "No thanks, Mom, I just grabbed a little bite. I would have fixed you a plate, but I thought you were taking a nap."

The lie rolls easily off your tongue and registers on your soul, and you feel huge shards of your morality begin to drift out of you. It dawns on your psyche that you have to take control of the situation and the woman's ability to inflict potentially mortal wounds on your soul. You also begin to understand that this situation, these feelings of anguish, have everything to do with you and nothing much to do with your beloved's (blankity blank) mother. You have to take the responsibility to make the change. You realize with startling clarity that you have only *One Life to Live,* and you have to live it on your own terms.

As you crawl back under the covers, feeling truly miserable inside and out, you realize that unless you change your way of thinking about that in-law person, you are doomed to spend the rest of the *Days of Your Life* in that "too warm" place rather than reclining in the heaven of your own making. You close your eyes and seek the *Guiding Light* that will take you back to a place of peace and sanity and honesty. Lo and behold, the light guides you right to that wonderful store where you can buy everything, including the nanny camcorder you knew you would need one day soon. Let her try to wiggle out of this one!

A sense of disquiet settles over you as you begin to see that unless you can find a way to love this woman as you love her offspring, you could end up in a *General Hospital.* You know a change must come, and it must start within you. You realize that you had better find that *Bold and Beautiful* person within you, and fast. For a brief moment, you feel that the only way to make this happen is to develop the level of personal honesty that will allow you to say to your dearly beloved, "Darling, you know I love you, and I know that you love me, and I know that you love your mother, and I am working on that too. However, could I work on it from another state?"

Pausing, you realize that in order to begin to love her, some things have to change. You recognize that you cannot continue to run away from the woman or the situation, and you cannot depend on her to change and to provide for your happiness. At this point, you make the final decision, the decision to help everyone else, especially your beloved, see for themselves what you have been seeing, hearing, and enduring all along. Tomorrow would be the day for a trip to Target for the nanny camcorder you knew you would have to purchase one day soon anyway. Tomorrow would be the day when you would show the world that nanny camcorders worked wonders, even on prospective grandmas. No longer would she be able to terrorize you with her retractable fangs and horns. You were ready to be honest and ready to help her along the way to her own personal honesty. You smile a smile of contentment as you fully acknowledge that unless you change your attitude and stand your ground, unless you speak to your truth and find your peace, you will, at least for the near future, remain one of the *Young and Restless.*

With sheer delight you contemplate the evening when you would invite dear mom and your dearly beloved to join you in an evening of popcorn and movies—"Oops, oh dear, what is that in the video player? Honey, you haven't been watching movies without me, have you? Well, let's all have a little peek, shall we? I sure hope this movie doesn't have any ugly creatures with fangs and horns." But then you pause. The reality of what you are about to do slams into your heart and almost crushes you. What would this do to your sweetheart? Did he really need to see his mother in full form? You ask yourself just what this would mean for you. You acknowledge that despite her evil ways, she had somehow managed to raise this incredible man and his brothers, men who were phenomenal men and husbands.

Next, you contemplate with deep and profound honesty, the role you played in all of this. Then you ask yourself the even more important questions, *Why have I placed my happiness in the hands of this woman? Why have I allowed myself to be drawn into this misery?* You decide then and there that this drama was over, and you will find a way to shower this woman with kindness and love. This is one neighbor you will work hard at loving as you love yourself. You pledge that this love will radiate white hot and true from you, and then, if she couldn't stand the heat, she, not you, would simply have to get the hell out of your kitchen.

Chapter 11

Friendship: The Breeding Ground of a Host of "Undocumented" Sins.

You can't get to heaven if you tell your number one "best friend" you are on the phone with your sick mother when you are really on the phone with your other number one "best friend" talking about her behind her back.

Why?

Let's Be Honest . . .

. . . 'cause sometimes three-way connect works when it's not supposed to!

When was the last time you heard the statement, "Oh, let me tell you what I just saw," or "You'll never believe what I just heard," or "Did you see that?" and it wasn't eventually followed by "God, I wish I had kept my big mouth shut?"

Chatty: "Hey Patsy, It's me, Chatty. Girl, did you see what our friend wore to the party last night?"

Patsy: "Who, Dorcas?"

Chatty: "No, not Dorcas. No, no, I'm talking 'bout our friend, Liz. Did you get a load of that awful outfit? You know, that girl needs to shed at least

20 pounds. She looked like a beached whale. And those poor shoes! They were begging for mercy under all that pressure. And you know they were two sizes too small. And who was that loser she was with?"

Patsy: "You mean the dude wearing the loud, pin-stripe, nineteen-seventies, pimped out Zoot suit?"

Chatty: "Yeah, yeah. Isn't he the dude who got sent up on fraud charges? When did he get out? I know she's my friend, but God, that girl's a loser."

Patsy: "I know what you mean. She sure needs some help, but I'm not taking on that project."

Chatty: "Oh, hold on. Let me get the other line."

Chatty: "Oh hey, Liz. What's up, girl? Girlfriend, you sure looked hot last night. Where did you get that fabulous dress? And those shoes! You have to let me borrow them sometime. But look, I'm on the other line with my mom. She's not doing so well. Let me get off with her, and I'll call you right back 'cuz girl, we gotta talk about our friend, Patsy. Did you see what that girl was wearing last night? But, listen, I gotta run. Catch up with you soon."

Chatty: "Hey Patsy, you'll never guess who was on the other line. Girl, it was that loser Liz . . ."

I can just see the puzzled look on your face, and hear the questions running through your confused mind, "When did dissing your friends become a sin? Which commandment am I breaking?" I can even imagine you flipping to the appendices in the back of the book just to be sure you haven't missed something. You're thinking to yourself, "Not another one. Isn't this hard enough already?" Well, no. It isn't. I'm afraid there are just a few hundred more that we haven't touched on yet, but which, as it turns out, are just as dastardly as the ten Thou

Shalt Nots and the Seven Deadlies. I will refer to these here as the UDSs, the "Undocumented Sins," or the "Oops, I was just joking" sins. Why? Because that is generally what we say when we get caught committing one of them (see Appendix 3 for a partial listing of these sins.)

For example, what happens when you, dear gossip, switch over from Liz back to Patsy and, lo and behold, you have accidentally established a three-way connection? As poor Liz sits silently listening to you and Patsy destroy her emotionally, she can't control the intake of breath and the sniffles. Tears streaming down her cheeks, she listens to her "best friends" annihilate her. Your response when you finally realize your grave error is? That's right "Oops, girl, we were just joking. You know we didn't mean it." So exactly what didn't you mean? Perhaps you didn't mean to *criticize* her clothing, her shoes, her size? Oh, that was just a joke. Or perhaps you really didn't mean to *gossip* about her behind her back with your "other best friend?" That too was just a joke. Perhaps you didn't mean to *judge* her choice of men. That was just another little joke. Or is it that, perhaps, you didn't mean to be a *hypocrite* when you pretended to be her friend. But maybe, just maybe, pretending to be her friend was actually the biggest joke of all.

We all know that the Bible admonishes against lying, cheating, stealing, and those other popular, well-known, and definitely overused sins. But, what about those other less obvious acts of missing the mark? What of the other sins that Moses didn't jot down, or perhaps, were listed on the first clay tablet he smashed to smithereens when he got ticked off at his relatives? You know how it is with family. But wait a minute now. Now that we have a moment to reflect, wasn't that Deadly Sin 7, the anger thing, that Moses committed? Do you think maybe that's why he didn't get to see the Promised Land—land of milk, honey, and all that other good stuff—with the rest of his kin? But no, those Deadly Sins didn't really surface until way after the Thou Shalt Nots. Anyway, forgive me. I digress. The question is, can we get away with these sins just because they are not included in a list somewhere? And, if they are mentioned in the Bible, just what does it say about them?

Let's start with a few of the ones of which we know we are all guilty. For example, gossiping (aka tattling or tale bearing). Solomon the Wise had a few choice words on the subject: "Without wood a fire goes out; without gossip a quarrel dies down." (Prov. 26:20).

He also cautioned in Prov. 26:22, "The words of a tattler are as wounds, and they go down into the innermost part of the body." For those among us of the non-Bible-thumping variety, there are many other worldly but wise admonitions against the heinous act of gossip. Consider the wisdom of an old Spanish Proverb that cautions: "Whoever gossips to you will gossip about you," or the Chinese Proverb that warns us: "What is told in the ear of a man is often heard 100 miles away."

To those of us who seek to criticize others in our random acts of gossiping, an unknown writer penned these insightful words; "When we judge or criticize another person, it says nothing about that person; it merely says something about our own need to be critical." Alice Duer Miller warns us: "If it's very painful for you to criticize your friends - you're safe in doing it. But if you take the slightest pleasure in it, that's the time to hold your tongue."

Regardless of which of the following wise men, Dale Carnegie or Benjamin Franklin, stated the following words, the advice remains true, "Any fool can criticize, condemn, and complain, and most fools do." H. Jackson Brown suggested, "Let the refining of your own life keep you so busy that you have little time to criticize others."

The following words did not come from the Bible, but from a wise woman of our time, Raisa M. Gorbachev: "Hypocrisy, the lie, is the true sister of evil, intolerance, and cruelty." Even the Bible cautions against hypocrites: "An hypocrite with his mouth destroyeth his neighbor. . . ." (Prov. 11:9).

Now, what of that popular act of judging others that we all seem to fall into so unconsciously? In the New Testament, Jesus cautions us: "Do not judge, or you too will be judged. For in the same way you judge others, you will be judged, and with the measure you use, it will be measured to you." Matthew 7:1-2

For those among us who do not seek our words of wisdom from the "Good Book," consider the words of Lawrence G. Lovasik, who suggested that: "It is just as cowardly to judge an absent person as it is wicked to strike a defenseless one. Only the ignorant and narrow-minded gossip, for they speak of persons instead of things."

One of our current wise authors and teachers, Wayne Dyer notes: "Judgments prevent us from seeing the good that lies beyond appearance," while the late Mother Teresa of Calcutta believed: "If you judge people, you have no time to love them."

The question that needs to be asked here is this: Is it the people that we are judging, and criticizing, and gossiping about whom we do not love, or is it ourselves? What leads us into these unkind acts, and especially toward those whom we profess to love? Carl Gustav Jung may have hit on something when he said that: "Everything that irritates us about others can lead us to an understanding of ourselves." So, do we ever stop to ask ourselves how many quarrels we have started and how many wounds we have inflicted with our gossiping? How many of our neighbors have we destroyed with our hypocrisy? Can we even begin to imagine what will be measured out to some of us based on what we have measured out to others with our judgments?

I imagine many of us have never stopped to consider how much damage we have inflicted on others as we indulge in a moment of hilarity at someone else's expense or in a moment of careless joking. The Bible even has a word about that! "Like a madman shooting firebrands or deadly arrows is a man who deceives his neighbor and says 'I was only joking'" (Prov. 26:18). Can you believe those smart Bible folks actually thought of that one? Seriously, I am willing to bet that in a moment of soul-searching and personal honesty, we will all discover that while these acts of missing the mark are not written down on anyone's list, they are indeed inscribed on our hearts under our very own list of Thou Shalt Nots.

Let's face it. We all know when we have missed the mark. We all know how badly most of us feel when we commit one of the Seven Deadlies or break one of the Thou Shalt Nots. We all know the private pain and disgust we feel when we get caught. We all know that, documented or not, our acts of *judgment, criticism, gossip, and hypocrisy* make us feel lousy inside. However, what happens when there is no one there to catch us but ourselves? Who will remind us that we have missed the mark? Who will set our standards of personal honesty? Who will be our heaven's gatekeepers, if not ourselves?

We all know how our bad behavior starts, but how does it end? Lawrence G. Lovasik suggested that, "Only a kind person is able to judge another justly and to make allowances for his weaknesses. A kind eye, while recognizing defects, sees beyond them." Perhaps that is where we can start. With an act of kindness toward those we are supposed to love. The Bible tells us that:

"Love is patient, love is kind.
It does not envy, it does not boast, it is not proud.
It is not rude, it is not self-seeking.
It is not easily angered, it keeps no record of wrongs.
Love does not delight in evil, but rejoices with the truth.
It always protects, always trusts, always hopes, always perseveres.
Love never fails."

I Cor. 13:4-8

Elizabeth Kubler-Ross, the famous psychologist, tells us: "The ultimate lesson all of us have to learn is unconditional love, which includes not only others but ourselves as well." Isn't it enlightening that it all seems to come back to Jesus' two simple

Commandments to:

". . . love the Lord your God with all your heart and with all your soul and with all your mind." And, to "love your neighbor as yourself."

Matt. 22: 37-39

Chapter 12

Party Hearty Saturday Night, Holy Roller Come Morning Light

You can't get to heaven trying to rinse off the smell of booze with holy water!

Why?
Let's Be Honest . . .

. . . 'cause the way some of us behave, it might take a bath in fire and brimstone to clean us up.

Sunday morning in a church, Hallelujah! Ladies and gentlemen, believe me when I say, there is absolutely no place on earth from which to bear witness to some of the greatest demonstrations of pride, envy, gluttony, lust, anger, greed, backbiting, deception, judgment, and just plain downright hating, than in church on a fine Sunday morning. However, brothers and sisters, all this sinning doesn't start there, and it is not restricted to the congregation. Can I get an Amen!?

Let's take a trip back to the mall where all the rule-breaking and downright bad behavior began. This time, let's bypass the shoe store where we have already acknowledged that we sacrificed the greater part of our soul. For this foray down the slippery slopes to hell, let's amble on down to our favorite department store.

Here, we will begin the quest for our ultimate external display of decadence. Here, the hunt ensues for the perfect outfit that will outdo whatever Sister so and so or Brother so and so, with their showoff selves, will stride in wearing come tomorrow morning. One thing we know for sure is that, come hell or high water, we will be outshining, outglitzing, and outblinging them and their high-stepping friends, even at the cost of our very souls!

When we enter the hallowed halls of that most sacrosanct of places come tomorrow, we must be confident that the outfit is shinier, the label more exclusive, and the makeup so impeccable that the most renowned beauty consultant will look at us in awe. Ladies, for us, the purse must make Gucci, Oscar, Dooney, and even Kate, weep with joy. The hat, if we dare to hide the elaborate "do," must boast more feathers than the flashiest peacock in the zoo. For all, brothers and sisters alike, the jewelry must make even Cartier drool with envy. But to what end?

I have searched high and low, in and out, and nowhere have I been able to find the dress code for entry into church, much less into heaven. Nowhere in the Good Book is it elaborated on, and as a matter of fact, rumor has it that somewhere in that same Good Book (Eccl. 5:15), it actually says "naked thou comest and naked thou will return." Nowhere is the value of this ritual—all the effort we take to make this weekly pilgrimage to the sacred place covered in glitz and glamour—documented. We have all heard the tales of the horror show that took place when Sister So and So walked in wearing the same dress or hat as the other Sister So and So and didn't even show the common decency of getting it in another color. God forbid God should see us so similarly clad. How on earth would he ever be able to tell us apart?

Now, please do not get me wrong. By no means am I suggesting that naked might be a better alternative to the shameful display of decadence and indecency many of us perpetrate in church on Sunday morning. What I am trying to determine here is the *why* of it all—why the need for the shameless profligacy and impropriety come Sunday morning? Can we engage in a moment of personal honesty and acknowledge that perhaps it is because of the line of thinking that goes something like this?

Mattie: "Clara, what are you wearing to church tomorrow? You know, it's Deaconess Recognition Day, and we have to be sharp!"

Clara: "Oh, Mattie, I don't know. But what I do I know is that I have nothing in this closet to wear. Wanna take a run to the mall?"

Mattie: "Well, I have to get my hair done at 1:00, but I'll meet you at 3:00. And you know we have to pick up something for the guys too. We can't have them looking tacky and have people thinking we don't care about them."

Clara: "You are sooooo right girl. See you soon. But Mattie wait, I'm gonna need to stop by the shoe store for a minute; wanna meet me there instead?"

Mattie: "Oh no girl, I already committed that sin, er, I mean, I already made that run yesterday, and I don't have any more commandments left to break. I mean, I don't have any more space in my closet for another pair of shoes."

Clara: "Are you taking your credit cards?"

Mattie: "Are you out of your mind? You know if I try to use any of those cards, they're gonna come and get me and take me straight to jail. No girl, the mortgage isn't due for a few more days, so I'm gonna take a loan out of that money. Then I'm gonna pray and ask the Good Lord to provide a way."

I don't know about you, but I could swear I heard the Deadly Sins of pride and greed shrieking with laughter and rearing their ugly heads in the midst of that brief exchange. Not to mention the sounds of glee coming from the many Thou Shalt Nots being broken, as in the lie, Thou Shalt Not 9, dear Clara told when she claimed that she had nothing in the closet she could consider wearing, or the robbery, Thou Shalt Not 8, Mattie committed when she used her mortgage money to shop for clothes she didn't need and couldn't afford. All of this, and we haven't even left the house as yet. There is more to come. You see, it's Saturday evening at the mall, and all is well. We are bursting at the seams with the fruits of our overindulgence, but we are by no means satiated.

Do we dare indulge in another moment of personal honesty and admit that our need for more and more continues to lead us, like cattle, steered by a ring through the nose? We seem to be wandering though life, slack-jawed and hollow-eyed, in constant need of more stimulation, more bragging rights, more "stuff." More, more, more! But, after all, it's Saturday night, why stop with a trip to the mall when there is a full night of glorious debauchery and frivolity waiting ahead. Why not aim for the sky with a trip out on the town? Are we joking here? You know we need something special to wear. God knows that nothing in the closet could possibly suffice!

So off we go. Out for a night full of self-indulgence, scandalous thrills, drink, food, and heaven knows what else await us. Who cares? After all, church doesn't start 'til 10 a.m.! But wait, is that the good Rev. Brother So and So that we just drove by in that dark car? Isn't that him sitting on the corner talking to that "Lady" in the fishnet stockings, the six-inch heels, and the glitter eyeliner? Noooooo, not the Good Reverend Dr. So and So. It just can't be!

Yes, brothers and sisters, it certainly can. Let's pause for a moment and reflect on the last few incidents of church leader frailty we have encountered in our media, a source that seems constantly ready to expose the reprehensible deeds of some of our most Holy Reverend Fathers. I mean those kindly, humble, giving, pious, three-piece linen-suited, silk handkerchief-flaunting, diamond-encrusted pinkie ring-wearing, brand-new latest model Lexus-driving preachers who show up on Sunday morning ready to castigate us for our missed marks of the past week.

Good Book in hand, these preachers stare down at us from the pulpit. Instinctively, yet with seemingly profound conviction, they quote the Bible, chapter by chapter, and verse by verse. The words of the commandments roll like oil off their silky, smooth tongues while they exhort us to avoid the temptations of lust, greed, pride and envy, all the while considering just how much of a take they will have in this Sunday's pledge for the ubiquitous building fund, aka the Reverend's (in)discretionary fund. Then, with seeming piety and stern faces, they wait for us to accept their invitation to join them at the altar, ready to confess our sins and ask forgiveness.

Sweat pours profusely from contorted faces as fingers jab accusatorily into empty air. Bodies move rhythmically to the beat of the drums, guitar, and piano while the choir behind them writhes in the seeming throes of ecstasy. Simultaneously, our generous spiritual leaders graciously offer us redemption while praying inwardly that no one caught their latest acts of indiscretion on videotape or that the next baby born to Sister So and So won't have the telltale signs of their oversized forehead or their obvious facial twitch like the last one did.

Perhaps, if we were to listen hard enough or pay a bit more attention, we may discover that the Right Reverend's rants and raves are actually born of his own personal pain and grief. What may be passing as righteous passion could just as well be the internal agony from his own wellspring of missed marks. So when do these pastors begin their own prayers for personal redemption, a process that can only be achieved through personal honesty? When do we begin to pray for our spiritual leaders?

Somewhere, it is said that evil men hide their deeds in darkness. If that is true, then it seems that Sunday morning is when all these deeds and their perpetrators crawl out of the darkness and rise to the surface waiting for absolution, so that they can prepare to start all over again next week. We know where it starts, of course, at the shoe store in the mall, but where does it end? Where do we go to begin the search for the only thing that can save us from total and complete destruction? How do we stem the pain from the loss of all that is of true value in this time of utter uncertainty and the seemingly inevitable loss of everything we hold dear?

Is our redemption and path to heaven in this hallowed space? Is church the place that should provide us with ultimate solace and peace? Is it in church that we can begin to leave the noise and crowds behind and begin a journey toward joy and happiness through the path of personal honesty? I say no. Not unless we first change ourselves by engaging in the life-affirming process of establishing personal honesty before we even enter the doors of our worship spaces. You see friends; it is not in church alone that we can discover that the true reason behind our mindless search for external fulfillment is that we are so empty on the inside. It is not in church alone that we can truly begin to look at our souls rather than at what Sister So and So or Brother So and So are wearing or driving. It is not in church alone that we decide against sharing our bodies and hearts with someone who belongs to someone else. It is not in church alone that we can gain a full appreciation of the two Commandments of Jesus to, "Love the Lord thy God with all thy soul and with all thy heart," and to "love thy neighbor as thy self." It is not in church alone that we determine that the "Seven Heavenly Virtues" of faith, hope, charity, fortitude, justice, temperance, and prudence would serve us far more than the Seven Deadly Sins. It is not in church alone that we can begin to discover the heavenly kingdom of God that is within us. It is not in this place alone that we can discover that we are truly perfect creatures created in the image and likeness of our God.

It is indeed only through the process of personal honesty as a first step that we will become the people we hope to be in our houses of worship and in our personal heavens here on earth—people who understand, embrace, and are even able to teach the words we aspire to live by. The task begins and ends with us.

Part 2

Covering All The Bases

Chapter 13

Can I Get An Amen?

Trust me when I say, you can get to heaven wearing flip flops and a bathrobe.

Why?

Let Be Honest . . .

. . . 'cause flip flops and a bathrobe can be haute couture when we truly know who we are!

We've all heard the saying, "good girls get to go to heaven, but bad girls have all the fun." Well folks, they lied to us! The truth is that there are no "good girls" or "bad girls" and no heaven or hell waiting to "go to." However, let's take a moment to examine the proposition. First, the beginning of the statement proposes that there is a heaven and a hell created by someone or something, who has the power to determine the outcome of our life. The second part of the statement that we need to consider is that this heaven and hell are somewhere out there, and we have to work to get there. What are the implications here? First, it appears that someone other than ourselves gets to determine our destiny. Second, we can never enjoy the fruits of our mortal labor (be it physical or spiritual) until we leave this mortal plane and ascend or descend to some other place where we will be judged by the Big Guy with the Big Book or the Little Guy with the Sin O'Meter. Boy, do I have big news for you!

It would appear that God, the creator of earth and of heaven, that place that used to be somewhere up in the sky, has bought some new real estate. Word from one of the most credible sources out there on the street, is that heaven can now be found right inside of you. "Know ye not that your body is the temple of the Holy Ghost which is in you?" (1 Cor. 6:19). Actually, this source tells us that it's been right there all along, right inside of us waiting to be inhabited. This source also tells us that the only other inhabitant on this piece of real estate is our Creator, waiting for us to come home and sit down for a meal and some good conversation, "And behold, I am with thee, and will keep thee in all places whither thou goest" (Gen. 28:15).

Imagine, you could be there right now, in your personal heaven, enjoying all the milk, honey, cheesecake, and carbs as we speak. We will never again need to overeat in order to be filled, and we will never gain an ounce, anyway, because all our inner spaces will be filled with joy and abundance, bliss and light. "If you are filled with light, with no dark corners, then your whole life will be radiant, as though a floodlight [1] is shining on you" (Luke 11:36).

You could be in your personal heaven knowing that you will never need to take from another to satisfy your needs because your loving provider is already there ready to give you all[2] good and perfect gifts. "It is your Father's pleasure to give you the kingdom" (Luke 12:32). You will never be lonely for a friend

[2] Imagine my surprise when I discovered that they had floodlights in biblical times. For confirmation see *Holy Bible: New Living Translation.* (1996). Tyndale House Publishers, Inc.

or a lover because you will have your friend as your constant companion "If you live in Me and My words remain in you and continue to live in your heart, ask whatever you will, and it shall be done for you" (John 15:7).

You will never need to wrap yourself in external garments to appear beautiful to the outside world or to yourself because your permanent housemate knows you as you truly are and knows how beautiful you are inside and out. 1 Peter 3:3-4 even cautions us to "Let not yours be the [merely] external adorning with [elaborate] interweaving and knotting of the hair, the wearing of jewelry, or changes of clothes; but let it be the inward adorning and beauty of the hidden person of the heart, with the incorruptible and unfading charm of a gentle and peaceful spirit, which [is not anxious or wrought up, but] is very precious in the sight of God."

You see, in our ideal, perfect heaven, the one of our own creation, we are utter perfection. In our perfect heaven, we do not become the thing we fear because fear has no power over us "For God has not given us a spirit of fear and timidity, but of power, love, and self-discipline" (2 Tim. 1:7). So we ask ourselves, "When all the fun and laughter is over, and the real work begins, how do I start this journey? What does it truly mean to be personally honest, and how do I get there from here?" The answer is really just as simple as slipping on that pair of flip-flops and putting on that bathrobe. The answer is simple, because we don't even have to leave home to find it. It is not at the mall, where we will be tempted with too-tight shoes. It is not in the ice cream shop, where we think love resides. It is not at the office, where we will be tempted with paper clips, blank checks, or another person's partner. It is not with our children, where we will be tempted to love them to death. And most definitely, it is not in the church on Sunday morning where chances are we will spend our time wishing we could rewind the clock to before last night or last year. Where is the answer? The answer is right where you are, right now, right in your heart and right in your very own mind. You see, it begins and ends with your own thoughts and your own reality, those thoughts that determine your behavior and lead you into wearing tight shoes in the first place.

If we see ourselves as living with God in perfect joy, bliss, and abundance, that vision becomes our truth, and nothing and no one can rob us of that reality. Folks, here is the best news of all. In our perfect heaven, we will never, and I mean never, ever, need to wear another pair of tight shoes because our best and closest friend, the one who created us in his image and likeness and who lives there with us, has seen our naked feet, bunions, corns, messed-up pinkie toe, jacked-up big toe, and all. So friends, put on the flip flops, or better still, run barefooted through life. God knows our true shoe size and loves us anyway.

Can I get an Amen?

Chapter 14

The Cheat Sheets--Oops, I Mean The Easy Reference Guides For The Care And Nurturance Of Your Precious Soul.

Why?

Let's Be Honest . . .

'Cause the work never ceases!

Appendix 1

For The Care And Nurturance Of Your Precious Soul:

Easy Reference Guide To The Ten "Thou Shalt Nots"

1. *Thou shalt have no other Gods before me.*

2. *Thou shalt not make for yourself an idol in the form of anything in heaven above or on earth beneath or in the waters below. Thou shalt not bow down to them or worship them.*

3. *Thou shalt not misuse the name of the Lord your God.*

4. *Thou shalt not forget the Sabbath day by forgetting to keep it holy. For on the seventh day, you shall not work.*

5. *Thou shalt not dishonor your father and your mother.*

6. *Thou shalt not murder.*

7. *Thou shalt not commit adultery.*

8. *Thou shalt not steal.*

9. *Thou shalt not give false testimony.*

10. *Thou shalt not covet your neighbor's house, or his wife, or his ass.*

Appendix 2

For The Care And Nurturance Of Your Precious Soul:

Easy Reference Guide To The Seven Deadlies

1. *Pride*
2. *Envy*
3. *Gluttony*
4. *Lust*
5. *Anger*
6. *Greed*
7. *Sloth*

Appendix 3

For The Care And Nurturance Of Your Precious Soul:

Easy Reference Guide To A Host Of Undocumented Sins

- *Gossip aka Backbiting* (As in "Thou Shalt Not talk about your friend, or your enemy, behind their backs or anywhere else for that matter.")

- *Hypocrisy & more Backbiting* (As in "Thou Shalt Not *pretend* to be my friend behind my back or in front of my face or anywhere else for that matter.")

- *Criticism* (As in "Thou Shalt Not talk badly about your friends to your other friends, behind their backs and preface the backbiting with the statement 'you know I love her dearly and would never do anything to hurt her, but . . .' ")

- *Judgment* (As in "Thou shalt Not compare your perfect behavior to anyone else's imperfect behavior unless you have first taken a keen look at your own behavior aka those who live in glass houses should never throw stones!")

- *Deceit* (As in "Thou Shalt Not undertake any activity which would lead you to defend yourself by beginning with the statement 'I know what you think, but this is not really what it looks like'. . . and ends with the statement 'please give me a chance to explain.'")

- *Lack of Integrity* (As in "Thou Shalt Not begin any action with the thought, 'I know I really shouldn't do this, but, it's just this one time. . .' ")

- *Boasting* (As in "Thou Shalt Not begin any sentence with the phrase "You know, I really don't mean to brag, but . . .")

- *Malice* (As in Thou shalt Not put thyself in a pickle by making the following statement: 'I know that the Good Book says to forgive and forget, but I'm not sure I can manage that on this occasion.")

- *Ugliness* (As in "Thou Shalt Not forget that ugly is as ugly does, and GOD DON'T LIKE UGLY!")

Appendix 4

For The Care And Nurturance Of Your Precious Soul:

Easy Reference Guide To Jesus' Two Commandments

1. *"You must love the Lord your God with all your heart, all your soul, and all your mind. This is the first and greatest commandment. A second is equally important.*

2. *Love your neighbor as yourself. All the other commandments and all the demands of the prophets are based on these two commandments."*

Appendix 5

For The Care And Nurturance Of Your Precious Soul:

Easy Reference Guide To The Seven Heavenly Virtues

1. *Faith*
2. *Hope*
3. *Charity*
4. *Fortitude*
5. *Justice*
6. *Temperance*
7. *Prudence*

Celtic Symbol for Love

Honesty begins with seeing the truth within.

Bibliography

Adinka Symbols of West Africa www.adinkra.org/htmls/adinkra/gyen.htm

Chalicewellayurveda http://www.chalicewellayurveda.com/web//images/stories/Love_Symbol.jpg

Holmes, Ernest. (1996). *The science of mind: A philosophy, a faith, a way of life.* New York: NY. Jeremy P. Tarcher/Putnam

Holy Bible: New Living Translation. (1996). Tyndale House Publishers, Inc. Weaton, IL.

Merriam-Webster's Collegiate Dictionary. (2006). Eleventh Edition. Merriam-Webster, Incorporated. Springfield, MA.

Michaels, Chris. (2003). *Your soul's assignment.* Kansas City: MO. Awakening World Enterprises.

Princeton University Blog Service www.blogs.princeton.edu

Ruiz, D. M. (1997). *A practical guide to personal freedom: The four agreements.* San Rafael: CA. Amber-Allen Publishing.

The Amplified Bible: Containing the Amplified Old Testament and the Amplified New Testament. (1987). Zondervan Bible Publishers, Grand Rapids, MI.

The Lyrics Library – The Lyrics Collection – Peter Gordon. P. Spector. To Know You is to Love you. http://www.mathematik.uniulm.de/paul/lyrics/petergordon/knowyo~1.html

The Seven Deadly Sins whitestonejournal.com/seven deadly sins/

Thinkexist.com www.thinkexist.comThis Little Light of Mine Official Site of Negro Spirituals www.negrospirituals.com/news.../this_**little_light_of_mine**.htm

Wisdom Quotes www.wisdomquotes.com/cat_hypocrisy.html

Zibu Language of the Angels http://www.languageofzibu.com/HonestyInfo.html

About The Author

Photo by:
Bashire Gavriel
www.kaizenimagery.com

Patricia St. E. Darlington, Ph.D.

Patricia St. E. Darlington, Ph.D., is a writer and college professor who has dedicated her life to helping others reach their greatest potential. Dr. Darlington is an Associate Professor of Intercultural Communication at Florida Atlantic University in Boca Raton, Florida.

Dr. Darlington is the founder of the Not-for Profit organization

Life Skills Academy, which is dedicated to the personal and social development of youth in order to create competent, effective, productive, global citizens, and *Life Skills Training and Consulting, Inc,* which provides services for corporations.

She is the co-author of the book entitled *Women, Power and Ethnicity: Working Toward Reciprocal Empowerment,* and the author of several scholarly journal articles. She has presented numerous workshops across the United States, in Hawaii and in West Africa, on the value of diversity, personal empowerment, and the power of women.

Dr. Darlington is an Ordained Non-Denominational Minister, and is the mother of three young adults, Bashir, Rolda, and Headley III. She lives in South Florida with her husband Headley II.

Contact Information:

pat@notightshoesinheaven.com

www.notightshoesinheaven.com